A POLITICAL PHILOSOPHY

A Political Philosophy

ROGER SCRUTON

continuum
LONDON • NEW YORK

Continuum UK
The Tower Building
11 York Road
London SE1 7NX

Continuum US
80 Maiden Lane
Suite 704
New York NY 10038

www.continuumbooks.com

First published 2006

British Library Cataloguing-in-Publication Data
A catalogue record for this book is available from the British Library.

ISBN: 0–8264–8036–5 (hb)
ISBN: 0–8264–9391–2 (pb)

Typeset by Kenneth Burnley, Wirral, Cheshire
Printed and bound in Great Britain by MPG Books Ltd, Bodmin, Cornwall

Contents

Introduction

English conservatism is rooted in the patrimony of the English upper class, in the quiet common sense of the old English constitution and in the plain-man unassuming practices that are, in the life of an English Tory, a handy substitute for thinking. My conservatism, by contrast, arose in reaction to May 1968 in France. It is an English reaction to continental posturing and is as rooted in high culture and highbrow books as the mumbo-jumbo of Althusser, Deleuze and Guattari. However, as I began to familiarize myself with the conservative literature I came to see that my situation is by no means a novel one, and had indeed been the exact position of Burke, who was stunned into articulating his beliefs, as I was, by a revolution in France. And Burke's response was imbued with the philosophical high-mindedness of the people he criticized. He gave a philosophical defence of the English settlement, against the unsettling effects of philosophy. He saw no greater danger in the French Revolution than the presumption that reasonable politics must be generated by rational thought. And by a *tour de force* of rational thought he justified the kind of politics that rational thought (he believed) puts in jeopardy.

There is, therefore, a kind of paradox at the heart of Burke's conservatism, and it is one that endures to this day. Conservatives in the British tradition are heirs to an island culture, in which custom prevails over reason as the final court of appeal. Their political process is governed by an unwritten constitution, whose principles are themselves a matter of custom rather than explicit rules. When interrogated as to the justice or reasonableness of any particular part of their inheritance – be it the common law, the monarchy, the nature and workings of parliament, the Anglican Church and its nonconformist offshoots – they tend either to shrug their shoulders, asserting that this is how things are because this is how they were, or else they take refuge in irony and self-mockery, confessing to the absurdity of a system whose principal merit is that nobody knows why it exists, and hence nobody knows quite why it shouldn't.

At the same time British conservatives are aware of the constant pressure of questions raised about their inheritance. The policy of accepting inherited customs and institutions as bedrock seemed reasonable enough in Burke's day, when the mass of citizens was not in a position to question them. But in a media-dominated democracy, in which affluence breeds choice and choice breeds doubt, the questions proliferate, and conservatives must contrive either to avoid them, or to address them in the language of mass communication. But the language of mass communication falls far short of the target. How can you justify the common law, for example – that intricate institution whereby law emerges from the conflicts that it resolves, rather than from the decisions of a sovereign power – in the language of the TV sitcom? How can you persuade the ordinary democratic man of the merits of the hereditary principle (as Burke called it), which seems to confer privileges on people who have never earned them, and to deny rewards to others who give of their best? It is scarcely surprising, in the light of that, if British conservatives have on the whole preferred to avoid discussion of their doctrines and to get on with the business of conserving things, even while pretending, like Margaret Thatcher, that they are following a progressive and 'modernizing' agenda in which freedom is the goal and the State the enemy.

However, there is a price to be paid for this pragmatic approach to politics. British Tories are becoming notorious for the thinness of their philosophy, the irresolution of their politics and their repeated failure to make an impact in the world of ideas. In bringing together the chapters that compose this book, I hope to mark out the areas in which philosophical thinking is needed, if the conservative position is to be intellectually persuasive. Conservatism, as I understand it, means the maintenance of the social ecology. Individual freedom is certainly a part of that ecology, since without it social organisms cannot adapt. But freedom is not the sole or the true goal of politics. Conservatism involves the conservation of our shared resources – social, material, economic and spiritual – and resistance to social entropy in all its forms.

Conservatism, in the eyes of its critics, will therefore seem to be doomed to failure, being no more than an attempt to escape the second law of thermodynamics. Entropy is always increasing, and every system, every organism, every spontaneous order will, in the long-term, be randomized. However, even if true, that does not make conservatism futile as a political practice, any more than medicine is futile, simply because 'in the long run we are all dead', as Keynes famously put it. Rather we should recognize the wisdom of Lord Salisbury's terse summary of his philosophy and accept that 'delay is life'. Conservatism is the politics of delay, the purpose of which is to maintain in being, for as long as possible, the life and health of a social organism.

Moreover, as thermodynamics also teaches us, entropy can be countered indefinitely at the local level, by injecting energy and exporting randomness. Conservatism emphasizes historical loyalties, local identities and the kind of long-term commitment that arises among people by virtue of their localized and limited affections. While socialism and liberalism are inherently global in their aims, conservatism is inherently local: a defence of some pocket of social capital against the forces of anarchic change. In this book, therefore, I have tried to mount a qualified defence of the nation state. National loyalty, I suggest, is a far securer foundation for addressing international problems – including those problems of environment and demography that threaten the future of the civilized world – than any system of global institutions. Whether or not readers agree with the positions that I advance, it is my hope that they will at least agree with me that the questions I discuss – neglected though they are by conservative politicians – are among the leading questions of modern politics.

Many chapters in this book are derived from published essays, although substantially revised and reduced in the course of assembling them. I list their sources in the Acknowledgements, and am grateful to the editors and publishers for their permission to revise the material for this collection.

Malmesbury
Christmas 2005

1

Conserving Nations

Democracies owe their existence to national loyalties – the loyalties that are supposedly shared by government and opposition, by all political parties and by the electorate as a whole. Wherever the experience of nationality is weak or non-existent democracy has failed to take root. For without national loyalty opposition is a threat to government, and political disagreements create no common ground. Yet everywhere the idea of the nation is under attack – either despised as an atavistic form of social unity, or even condemned as a cause of war and conflict, to be broken down and replaced by more enlightened and more universal forms of jurisdiction.

We in Europe stand at a turning point in our history. Our parliaments and legal systems still have territorial sovereignty. They still correspond to historical patterns of settlement that have enabled the French, the Germans, the Spaniards, the British and the Italians to say 'we' and to know whom they mean by it. The opportunity remains to recuperate the legislative powers and the executive procedures that formed the nation states of Europe. At the same time, the process has been set in motion that would expropriate the remaining sovereignty of our parliaments and courts, that would annihilate the boundaries between our jurisdictions, that would dissolve the nationalities of Europe in a historically meaningless collectivity, united neither by language, nor by religion, nor by customs, nor by inherited sovereignty and law. We have to choose whether to go forward to that new condition, or back to the tried and familiar sovereignty of the territorial nation state.

However, our political elites speak and behave as though there were no such choice to be made. They refer to an inevitable process, to irreversible changes, and, while at times prepared to distinguish a 'fast' from a 'slow' track into the future, they are clear in their minds that these two tracks lead to a single destination – the destination of transnational government, under a common system of law, in which national loyalty will be no more significant than support for a local football team.

My case is not that the nation state is the only answer to the problems of modern government, but that it is the only answer that has proved itself. We may feel tempted to experiment with other forms of political order. But experiments on this scale are dangerous, since nobody knows how to predict or to reverse the results of them. The French, Russian and Nazi Revolutions were bold experiments; but in each case they led to the collapse of legal order, to mass murder at home and to belligerence abroad. The wise policy is to accept the arrangements, however imperfect, that have evolved through custom and inheritance, to improve them by small adjustments, but not to jeopardize them by large-scale alterations the consequences of which nobody can really envisage. The case for this approach was unanswerably set before us by Burke in his *Reflections on the French Revolution*, and subsequent history has repeatedly confirmed his view of things. The lesson that we should draw, therefore, is that since the nation state has proved to be a stable foundation of democratic government and secular jurisdiction, we ought to improve it, to adjust it, even to dilute it, but not to throw it away.

The initiators of the European experiment – both the self-declared prophets and the behind-the-doors conspirators – shared a conviction that the nation state had caused the two world wars. A united states of Europe seemed to them to be the only recipe for lasting peace. This view is for two reasons entirely unpersuasive. First, it is purely negative: it rejects nation states for their belligerence, without giving any positive reason to believe that transnational states will be any better. Second, it identifies the normality of the nation state through its pathological versions. As Chesterton has argued about patriotism generally, to condemn patriotism because people go to war for patriotic reasons is like condemning love because some loves lead to murder. The nation state should not be understood in terms of the French nation at the Revolution or the German nation in its twentieth-century frenzy. For those were nations gone mad, in which the sources of civil peace had been poisoned and the social organism colonized by anger, resentment and fear. All Europe was threatened by the German nation, but only because the German nation was threatened by itself. Nationalism is part of the pathology of national loyalty, not its normal condition. Who in Europe has felt comparably threatened by the Spanish, Italian, Norwegian, Czech or Polish forms of national identity, and who would begrudge those people their right to a territory, a jurisdiction and a sovereignty of their own?

Left-liberal writers, in their reluctance to adopt the nation as a social aspiration or a political goal, sometimes distinguish nationalism from 'patriotism' – an ancient virtue extolled by the Romans and by those like Machiavelli who first made the intellectual case for modern secular jurisdiction.[1] Patriotism, they argue, is the loyalty of citizens, and the foundation of 'republican' government; nationalism is a shared hostility to the stranger, the intruder, the person who belongs 'outside'. I feel some sympathy for that approach. Properly understood, however, the republican patriotism defended by Machiavelli, Montesquieu and Mill is a *form* of national loyalty: not a pathological form like nationalism, but a natural love of country, countrymen and the culture that unites them. Patriots are attached to the people and the territory that are *theirs by right*; and patriotism involves an attempt to transcribe that right into impartial government and a rule of law. This underlying territorial right is implied in the very word – the *patria* being the 'fatherland', the place where you and I belong and to which we return, if only in thought, at the end of all our wanderings.

Territorial loyalty, I suggest, is at the root of all forms of government where law and liberty reign supreme. Attempts to

1 The distinction is carefully set out and defended by Maurizio Viroli, in *For Love of Country: An Essay on Patriotism and Nationalism*, Oxford: Clarendon Press, 1995.

denounce the nation in the name of patriotism therefore contain
no real argument against the kind of national sovereignty that I
shall be advocating.[2] I shall be defending what Mill called the
'principle of cohesion among members of the same community or
state', and which he distinguished from nationalism (or 'nationality, in the vulgar sense of the term'), in the following luminous
words:

> We need scarcely say that we do not mean nationality, in the
> vulgar sense of the term; a senseless antipathy to foreigners;
> indifference to the general welfare of the human race, or an
> unjust preference for the supposed interests of our own
> country; a cherishing of bad peculiarities because they are
> national, or a refusal to adopt what has been found good by
> other countries. We mean a principle of sympathy, not of
> hostility; of union, not of separation. We mean a feeling of
> common interest among those who live under the same
> government, and are contained within the same natural or
> historical boundaries. We mean, that one part of the commu-
> nity do not consider themselves as foreigners with regard to
> another part; that they set a value on their connexion – feel
> that they are one people, that their lot is cast together, that
> evil to any of their fellow-countrymen is evil to themselves,
> and do not desire selfishly to free themselves from their share
> of any common inconvenience by severing the connexion.[3]

The phrases that I would emphasize in that passage are these: 'our
own country', 'common interest', 'natural or historical boundaries' and '[our] lot is cast together'. Those phrases resonate with

---

2   The leading defender of a left-liberal patriotism is John Schaar. See especially
    'The Case for Patriotism', *American Review*, 17, May 1973 and *Legitimacy in
    the Modern State*, New Brunswick, NJ: Transaction Books, 1981. The case
    has been made in the context of English socialism by Hugh Cunningham, 'The
    Language of Patriotism, 1750–1915', *History Workshop*, 12, 1981, and elo-
    quently taken up by Maurizio Viroli, *op. cit.*
3   J. S. Mill, *A System of Logic* (tenth edn), London: Longmans, 1879, vol. 2,
    p. 522.

the historical loyalty that I shall be defending. To put the matter briefly: the case against the nation state has not been properly made, and the case for the transnational alternative has not been made at all. I believe, therefore, that we are on the brink of decisions that could prove disastrous for Europe and for the world, and that we have only a few years in which to take stock of our inheritance and to reassume it. Now more than ever do those words of Goethe's *Faust* ring true for us:

> *Was du ererbt von deinen Vätern hast,*
> *Erwirb es, um es zu besitzen.*

What you have inherited from your forefathers, earn it, that you might own it. We in the nation states of Europe need to earn again the sovereignty that previous generations so laboriously shaped from the inheritance of Christianity, imperial government and Roman law. Earning it, we will own it, and so be at peace within our borders.

Citizenship

Never in the history of the world have there been so many migrants. And almost all of them are migrating from regions where nationality is weak or non-existent to the established nation states of the West. They are not migrating because they have discovered some previously dormant feeling of love or loyalty towards the nations in whose territory they seek a home. On the contrary, few of them identify their loyalties in national terms and almost none of them in terms of the nation where they settle. They are migrating in search of citizenship – which is the principal gift of national jurisdictions, and the origin of the peace, law, stability and prosperity that still prevail in the West.

Citizenship is the relation that arises between the State and the individual when each is fully accountable to the other. It consists in a web of reciprocal rights and duties, upheld by a rule of law which stands higher than either party. Although the State enforces the law, it enforces it equally against itself and against the private citizen. The citizen has rights which the State is duty-bound to uphold, and also duties which the State has a right to enforce. Because these rights and duties are defined and limited by the law, citizens have a clear conception of where their freedoms end. Where citizens are appointed to administer the State, the result is 'republican' government.[4]

Subjection is the relation between the State and the individual that arises when the State need not account to the individual, when the rights and duties of the individual are undefined or defined only partially and defeasibly, and when there is no rule of law that stands higher than the State that enforces it. Citizens are freer than subjects, not because there is more that they can get away with, but because their freedoms are defined and upheld by the law. People who are subjects naturally aspire to be citizens, since a citizen can take definite steps to secure his property, family and business against marauders, and has effective sovereignty over his own life. That is why people migrate from the states where they are subjects, to the states where they can be citizens.

Freedom and security are not the only benefits of citizenship. There is an economic benefit too. Under a rule of law contracts can be freely engaged in and collectively enforced. Honesty becomes the rule in business dealings, and disputes are settled by courts of law rather than by hired thugs. And because the principle of accountability runs through all institutions, corruption can be identified and penalized, even when it occurs at the highest level of government.

Marxists believe that law is the servant of economics, and that 'bourgeois legality' comes into being as a result of, and for the sake of, 'bourgeois relations of production' (by which is meant the market economy). This way of thinking has been so influential that even today it is necessary to point out that it is the opposite

---

4　I adopt this definition in order to identify an ideal that has been defended in various forms by Aristotle, Machiavelli, Montesquieu, Kant and the American Founding Fathers. Republican government is not to be contrasted with monarchy (our own government is both), but with absolute rule, dictatorship, one-party rule and a host of other possibilities that fall short of participatory administration. Nor are republican governments necessarily democratic.

of the truth. The market economy comes into being because the rule of law secures property rights and contractual freedoms, and forces people to account for their dishonesty and for their financial misdeeds. That is another reason why people migrate to places where they can enjoy the benefit of citizenship. A society of citizens is one in which markets flourish, and markets are the precondition of prosperity.

A society of citizens is a society in which strangers can trust one another, since everyone is bound by a common set of rules. This does not mean that there are no thieves or swindlers; it means that trust can grow between strangers, and does not depend upon family connections, tribal loyalties or favours granted and earned. This strikingly distinguishes a country like Australia, for example, from a country like Kazakhstan, where the economy depends entirely on the mutual exchange of favours, among people who trust each other only because they also know each other and know the networks that will be used to enforce any deal.[5] It is also why Australia has an immigration problem, and Kazakhstan a brain-drain.

As a result of this, trust among citizens can spread over a wide area, and local baronies and fiefdoms can be broken down and overruled. In such circumstances markets do not merely flourish: they spread and grow, to become co-extensive with the jurisdiction. Every citizen becomes linked to every other, by relations that are financial, legal and fiduciary, but which presuppose no personal tie. A society of citizens can be a society of strangers, all enjoying sovereignty over their own lives, and pursuing their individual goals and satisfactions. Such are Western societies today. They are societies in which you form common cause with strangers, and which all of you, in those matters on which your common destiny depends, can with conviction say 'we'.

The existence of this kind of trust in a society of strangers should be seen for what it is: a rare achievement, whose pre-conditions are not easily fulfilled. If it is difficult for us to appreciate

---

5   See Francis Fukuyama, *Trust: The Social Virtues and the Creation of Prosperity*, New York: Free Press, 1995.

this fact it is in part because trust between strangers creates an illusion of safety, encouraging people to think that, because society ends in agreement, it begins in it too. Thus it has been common since the Renaissance for thinkers to propose some version of the 'social contract' as the foundation of a society of citizens. Such a society is brought into being, so Hobbes, Locke, Rousseau and others in their several ways argue, because people come together and agree on the terms of a contract by which each of them will be bound. This idea resonates powerfully in the minds and hearts of citizens, because it makes the State itself into just another example of the kind of transaction by which they order their lives. It presupposes no source of political obligation other than the consent of the citizen, and conforms to the inherently sceptical nature of modern jurisdictions, which claim no authority beyond the rational endorsement of those who are bound by their laws.

The theory of the social contract begins from a thought-experiment, in which a group of people gather together to decide on their common future. But if they are in a position to decide on their common future, it is because they already have one: because they recognize their mutual togetherness and reciprocal dependence, which makes it incumbent upon them to settle how they might be governed under a common jurisdiction in a common territory. In short, the social contract requires a relation of membership, and one, moreover, which makes it plausible for the individual members to conceive the relation between them in contractual terms. Theorists of the social contract write as though it presupposes only the first-person singular of free rational choice. In fact it presupposes a first-person plural, in which the burdens of belonging have already been assumed.

Membership and Nationality

It is because citizenship presupposes membership that nationality has become so important in the modern world. In a democracy governments make decisions and impose laws on people who are duty-bound to accept them. Democracy means living with strangers on terms that may be, in the short-term, disadvantageous; it means being prepared to fight battles and suffer losses on behalf of people whom one neither knows nor particularly wants to know. It means appropriating the policies that are made in one's name and endorsing them as 'ours', even when one disagrees with them. Only where people have a strong sense of who 'we' are, why 'we' are acting in this way or that, why 'we' have behaved rightly in one respect, wrongly in another, will they be so involved in the collective decisions as to adopt them as their own. This first-person plural is the precondition of democratic politics, and must be safeguarded at all costs, since the price of losing it is social disintegration.

Nationality is not the only kind of social membership, nor is it an exclusive tie. However, it is the only form of membership that has shown itself able to sustain a democratic process and a liberal rule of law. We should compare communities defined by nation with those defined by tribe or creed. Tribal societies define themselves through a fiction of kinship. Individuals see themselves as members of an extended family, and even if they are strangers this fact is only superficial, to be instantly put aside on discovery of the common ancestor and the common web of kin. Tribal societies tend to be hierarchical, with accountability running one way – from subject to chief – but not from chief to subject. The idea of an impartial rule of law, sustained in being by the very government that is subject to it, has no place in the world of kinship ties, and when it comes to outsiders – the 'strangers and sojourners' in the land of the tribe – they are regarded either as outside the law altogether and not entitled to its protection, or as protected by treaty. Nor can outsiders easily become insiders, since that which divides them from the tribe is an incurable genetic fault.

Tribal ideas survive in the modern world not merely because there are parts where they have never lost their hold on the collective imagination, but also because they provide an easy call to unity, a way of re-creating loyalty in the face of social breakdown. 'Racism' is a much abused word. A respectable definition of it, however, would be this: the attempt to impose a tribal idea of membership on a society that has been shaped in some other way.

This is what the Nazis attempted to do, and they were, in their way, successful. But their success was purchased at the cost of the political process, and the democracy which had brought them power vanished as soon as they acquired it.

Distinct from the tribe, but closely connected with it, is the 'creed community' – the society whose criterion of membership is religious. Those who worship my gods, and accept the same divine prescriptions, are joined to me by this, even though we are strangers. Creed communities, like tribes, extend their claims beyond the living. The dead acquire the privileges of the worshipper through the latter's prayers. But the dead are present in these new ceremonies on very different terms. They no longer have the authority of tribal ancestors; rather, they are subjects of the same divine overlord, undergoing their reward or punishment in conditions of greater proximity to the ruling power. They throng together in the great unknown, just as we will, released from every earthly tie and united by faith.[6]

The initial harmony between tribal and credal criteria of membership may give way to conflict, as the rival forces of family love and religious obedience exert themselves over small communities. This conflict has been one of the motors of Islamic history, and can be witnessed all over the Middle East, where local creed communities have grown out of the monotheistic religions and shaped themselves according to a tribal experience of membership.

It is in contrast with the tribal and credal forms of membership that the nation should be understood. By a nation I mean a people settled in a certain territory, who share language, institutions, customs and a sense of history and who regard themselves as equally committed both to their place of residence and to the legal and political process that governs it. Members of tribes see each other as a family; members of creed communities see each other as the faithful; members of nations see each other as neighbours.

6 I take the term 'creed community' from Spengler, and discuss what it means in *The West and the Rest*, London: Continuum, 2002.

Vital to the sense of nationhood, therefore, is the idea of a common territory, in which we are all settled, and to which we are all entitled as our home.

People who share a territory share a history; they may also share a language and a religion. The European nation state emerged when this idea of a community defined by a place was enshrined in sovereignty and law – in other words when it was aligned with a territorial jurisdiction. The nation state is, therefore, the natural successor to territorial monarchy, and the two may be combined, and often have been combined, since the monarch is so convenient a symbol of the trans-generational ties that bind us to our country.

Nations and Nationalism

Much learned ink has been spilled over the question of the nation and its origins. The theory that the nation is a recent invention, the creation of the modern administrative state, was probably first articulated by Lord Acton in a thin but celebrated article.[7] Writers from all parts of the political spectrum seem to endorse versions of this view, arguing that nations are bureaucratic inventions, whose emergence is inseparable from the culture of the written word.[8] Radicals use this fact to suggest that nations are transient, with no god-given right to exist or natural legitimacy, while conservatives use it to suggest the opposite, that nationality is an achievement, a 'winning through' to an order that is both more stable and more open than the old creed communities and tribal atavisms which it replaces.

---

7 J. E. E. Dalberg-Acton, first Baron Acton, 'Nationality', in *The History of Freedom and Other Essays*, eds J. N. Figgis and R. V. Lawrence, London: Macmillan, 1907.

8 Ernest Gellner, *Nations and Nationalism*, Oxford: Blackwell, 1983; Benedict Anderson, *Imagined Communities* (second edn), London: Verso, 1991; Eric Hobsbawm, *Nations and Nationalism since 1780*, Cambridge: CUP, 1990; Elie Kedourie, *Nationalism*, London: Hutchinson University Library, 1960; Kenneth Minogue, *Nationalism*, London: Batsford, 1967.

When it is said that nations are artificial communities, however, it should be remembered that there are two kinds of social artifact: those that result from a decision, as when two people form a partnership, and those that arise 'by an invisible hand', from decisions that in no way intend them. Institutions that arise by an invisible hand have a spontaneity and naturalness that may be lacking from institutions that are explicitly designed. Nations are spontaneous by-products of social interaction. Even when there is a conscious nation-building decision, the result will depend on the invisible hand. This is even true of the United States of America, which is by no means the entity today that the Founding Fathers intended. Yet the USA is the most vital and most patriotic nation in the modern world.

The example also illustrates Lord Acton's thesis. Nations are composed of neighbours, in other words of people who share a territory. Hence they stand in need of a territorial jurisdiction. Territorial jurisdictions require legislation, and therefore a political process. This process transforms shared territory into a shared identity. And that identity is the nation state. There you have a brief summary of American history: people settling together, solving their conflicts by law, making that law for themselves and, in the course of this process, defining themselves as a 'we', whose shared assets are the land and its law.

The 'invisible hand' process that was so illuminatingly discussed by Adam Smith depends upon, and is secretly guided by, a legal and institutional framework.[9] Under a rule of law, for example, the free interaction of individuals will result in a market economy. In the legal vacuum of post-communist Russia, however, this free interaction of individuals has produced a command economy in the hands of gangsters. Likewise the invisible hand that gave rise to the nation was guided at every point by the territorial law. This

9   See Adam Smith, *Inquiry into the Nature and the Causes of the Wealth of Nations*, 1776, and the discussion of 'invisible hand' explanations in Robert Nozick, *Anarchy, State and Utopia*, Oxford: Basil Blackwell, 1974. The invisible hand theory was generalized by F. A. Hayek to produce a comprehensive account of legal and institutional development, in *Law, Legislation and Liberty*, 2 vols, London: Routledge and Kegan Paul, 1976.

'law of the land' has been an important shaping force in English history, as Maitland and others have shown.[10] And it is through the process whereby land and law become attached to each other that true national loyalty is formed.

Now people cannot share territory without sharing many other things too: language, customs, markets and (in European conditions) religion. Hence every territorial jurisdiction will be associated with complex and interlocking loyalties of a credal and dynastic kind. However, it will also be highly revisionary of those loyalties. The law treats individuals as bearers of rights and duties. It recasts their relations with their neighbours in abstract terms; it shows a preference for contract over status and for definable interests over inarticulate bonds. It is hostile to all power and authority that is not exerted from within the jurisdiction. In short, it imprints on the community a distinctive political form. Hence when the English nation took shape in the late Middle Ages, it became inevitable that the English would have a church of their own, and that their faith would be defined by their allegiance, rather than their allegiance by their faith. In making himself head of the Church of England, Henry VIII was merely translating into a doctrine of law what was already a matter of fact.

At the same time, we must not think of territorial jurisdiction as merely a conventional arrangement: a kind of ongoing and severable agreement, of the kind that appealed to the social contract thinkers of the Enlightenment. It involves a genuine 'we' of membership: not as visceral as that of kinship; not as uplifting as that of worship, but for those very reasons more suited to the modern world and to a society of strangers in which faith is dwindling or dead.

A jurisdiction gains its validity either from an immemorial past, or from a fictitious contract between people who already *belong together*. Consider the case of the English. A settled jurisdiction, defined by territory, has encouraged us to define our rights and

---

10   F. W. Maitland, *The Constitutional History of England*, London: William Hodge & Co., 1908.

liberties and established from Saxon times a reciprocal accountability between 'us' and the sovereign who is 'ours'. The result of
this has been an experience of safety, quite different from that of
the tribe, but connected with the sense that we belong in this
place, and that our ancestors and descendents belong here too.
The common language – itself the product of territorial settlement
– has reinforced the feeling. But to suppose that we could have
enjoyed these territorial, legal and linguistic legacies, and yet
refrained from becoming a nation, representing itself to itself as
entitled to these things, and defining even its religion in terms of
them, is to give way to fantasy. In no way can the emergence of
the English nation, as a form of membership, be regarded as a
product of Enlightenment universalism, or the Industrial Revolution, or the administrative needs of a modern bureaucracy. It
existed before those things, and also shaped them into powerful
instruments of its own.

To put the matter simply: nations are defined not by kinship or
religion but by a homeland. Europe owes its greatness to the fact
that the primary loyalties of the European people have been
detached from religion and re-attached to the land. Those who
believe that the division of Europe into nations has been the
primary cause of European wars should remember the devastating wars of religion that national loyalties finally brought to an
end. And they should study our art and literature, which is an art
and literature not of war but of peace, an invocation of home and
the routines of home, of gentleness, everydayness and enduring
settlement. Its quarrels are domestic quarrels, its protests are
pleas for neighbours, its goal is homecoming and contentment
with the place that is ours. Even the popular culture of the
modern world is a covert re-affirmation of a territorial form of
loyalty. *The Archers, Neighbours, EastEnders*: all such mirrors of
ordinary existence are in the business of showing settlement and
neighbourhood, rather than tribe or religion, as the primary
social legacies.

People need to identify themselves through a first-person plural
if they are to accept the sacrifices required by society. And the first-
person plural of nationhood, unlike those of tribe or religion, is

intrinsically tolerant of difference.[11] It involves a discipline of neighbourliness, a respect for privacy and a desire for citizenship, in which people maintain sovereignty over their own lives and the kind of distance that makes such sovereignty possible. The 'clash of civilizations' which, according to Samuel Huntington, is the successor to the Cold War is, in my view, no such thing. It is a conflict between two forms of membership – the national, which tolerates difference, and the religious, which abhors it.[12]

But then, how do we explain the Terror in the French Revolution, the Holocaust, the Spanish civil war – to name but three modern horrors – if we do not see the nation as one part of the cause of them? This is where we should distinguish national loyalty from nationalism. National loyalty involves a love of home and a preparedness to defend it; nationalism is a belligerent *ideology*, which uses national symbols in order to conscript the people to war. When the Abbé Sieyès declared the aims of the French Revolution, it was in the language of nationalism: 'The nation is prior to everything. It is the source of everything. Its will is always legal. . . . The manner in which a nation exercises its will does not matter; the point is that it does exercise it; any procedure is adequate, and its will is always the supreme law'.[13] Those words express the very opposite of a true national loyalty. Not only do they involve an idolatrous deification of the 'Nation', elevating it far above the people of whom it is in fact composed. They do so in order to punish, to exclude, to threaten rather than to facilitate citizenship and to guarantee peace. The nation is here being deified, and used to intimidate its members, to purge the common home of those who are thought to pollute it. And the

---

11 See *The West and the Rest*, *op. cit*. See also Jonathan Sacks, *The Dignity of Difference*, London: Continuum Books, 2002, in which the Chief Rabbi defends the respect for cultural and religious difference that the nation state makes possible, and which vanishes when the only form of available membership is religious or tribal.

12 Samuel Huntington, *The Clash of Civilizations and the Remaking of World Order*, New York: Simon & Schuster, 1996.

13 E. Sieyès, *What is the Third Estate?*, tr. M. Blondel, ed. S. E. Finer, London: Pall Mall, 1963, pp. 124, 128.

way is being prepared for the abolition of all legal restraint, and the destruction of the territorial rule of law. In short, this kind of nationalism is not a national loyalty, but a religious loyalty dressed up in territorial clothes.

In every case we should distinguish nationalism and its inflammatory, quasi-religious call to re-create the world from national loyalty, of the kind that we know from our own historical experience.[14] Nationalism belongs to those surges of religious emotion that have so often led to European war. National loyalty is the explanation of that more durable, less noticeable and less interesting thing, which is European peace.

Our Constituent Nations

Since national loyalties are defined by territory, they can be multiple, and can nest within each other without conflict. In this they are manifestly unlike religious or tribal attachments, even when – as in the case of inherited monarchy – a vestige of tribal sentiment lingers on in symbolic form. Thus the union with Scotland occurred by a legal process whose effects could not be avoided, once James VI of Scotland had inherited the English crown. Even if other differences – kinship and religion – remained; and even if the idiolect of Scotland was a spur to separatist intentions; the British nation (which at first called itself an 'empire') was an inevitable result of the juridical process. It would be wrong to see this process as purely political, since the new state resulted from it and did not produce it. Moreover, the two jurisdictions have retained their own law and aimed for harmony rather than assimilation. The process should be seen for what it is: an accommodation of neighbours, whose geographical proximity, shared language and overlapping customs create a long-standing alliance between them. It is perfectly possible, therefore, for Scots to regard themselves as sharing their British nationality with the

---

14 On the religious nature of nationalist bellicosity see Adam Zamoyski, *Holy Madness: Romantics, Patriots and Revolutionaries, 1776–1871*, London: Phoenix, 1999.

English, even if they have another and more visceral nationality as Scots. For when loyalties are defined by territory, they can contain each other, just as territories do.

At the same time all British subjects – recent immigrants included – are heirs to the deep historical experience of England as a homeland and a territorial jurisdiction, a place of uninterrupted settlement under the rule of a common law. This law has long been recognized as possessing an authority higher than any individual or any government, and has shaped the character and the peculiar law-abidingness of British people, whether of Saxon or of Celtic descent.[15] Thanks to this territorial and legal inheritance, the British people can draw on a national identity that has shown itself more able to withstand shocks and acts of aggression than any other in Europe: the identity that is centred on England. To be British is to partake of that national identity. It is an identity that is permissive towards difference, and which allows other loyalties to nest within it and around it. And this is simply one instance of a great virtue in the national idea, and one that uniquely suits it to the troubled times in which we live.

Virtues of Nationality

We, as citizens of nation states, are bound by reciprocal obligations to all those who can claim our nationality, regardless of family, and regardless of faith. Hence freedom of worship, freedom of conscience, freedom of speech and opinion offer no threat to our common loyalty. Our law applies to a definite territory, and our legislators are chosen by those whose home it is. The law, therefore, confirms our common destiny and attracts our common obedience. Law-abidingness becomes part of the scheme of things, part of *the way in which the land is settled*. Our people can quickly unite in the face of threat, since they are uniting in

---

15 I have argued the point in *England: an Elegy*, London: Chatto and Windus, 2000. The idea of English law as standing above all powers within the State, including the sovereign, goes back to medieval times, being explicitly affirmed by the thirteenth-century judge, Henry de Bracton, in his *De legibus et consuetudinibus Angliae* of c. 1220.

defence of the thing that is necessary to all of them – their territory. The symbols of national loyalty are neither militant nor ideological, but consist in peaceful images of the homeland, of the place where we belong. National loyalties, therefore, aid reconciliation between classes, interests and faiths, and form the background to a political process based in consensus rather than in force. In particular, national loyalties enable people to respect the sovereignty and the rights of the individual.

For those and similar reasons, national loyalty does not merely *issue* in democratic government, but is profoundly assumed by it. People bound by a national 'we' have no difficulty in accepting a government whose opinions and decisions they disagree with; they have no difficulty in accepting the legitimacy of opposition, or the free expression of outrageous-seeming views. In short, they are able to live with democracy, and to express their political aspirations through the ballot box. None of those good things are to be found in states that are founded on the 'we' of tribal identity or the 'we' of faith. And in modern conditions all such states are in a constant state of conflict and civil war, with neither a genuine rule of law nor durable democracy.

The virtues of the nation state are revealed in two characteristics that are often cited by those who are most wedded to transnational governance: accountability and civil rights. Ever since Terence half-humorously asked the question – *quis custodiet illos custodes?* Who will guard those guardians? – the question of accountability has been at the forefront of all constructive political thinking. However benign the monarch, the ruling class or the 'vanguard party', there is no likelihood that he, she or they will remain benign for long, when answerable to no one but themselves. Government offers security to the citizens only if it is also accountable to them. Accountability is not brought into being merely by declaring that it exists, nor even by setting up institutions that theoretically enshrine it. It is brought into being when citizens are active in enforcing it. This requires the ability to mobilize opinion against the rulers, in such a way as to remove them from power. That in turn can occur only if citizens stand up for one another's right of protest, and recognize a common interest in allowing a voice to opposition. Citizens must co-operate in maintaining the institutions that will subject political decision-making to the scrutiny of a free press and a rule of law.

National loyalty is the rock on which all such attitudes are founded. It enables people to co-operate with their opponents, to agree to differ and to build institutions that are higher, more durable and more impartial than the political process itself. It enables people to live, in other words, in a depoliticized society, a society in which individuals are sovereign over their own lives yet confident that they will join together in defence of their freedoms, engaging in adversarial politics meanwhile.

The point is illustrated by recent experience of imposing democratic rule on countries sustained by no national loyalty. Almost as soon as democracy is introduced a local elite gains power, thereafter confining political privilege to its own gang, tribe or sect, and destroying all institutions that would force it to account to those that it has disenfranchised. This we have seen in the Middle East, in the Russian Empire and in Africa. Accountability to strangers is a rare gift and in the history of the modern world only the nation state and the empire centred on a nation state have really achieved it.

Moreover, every expansion of the jurisdiction beyond the frontiers of the nation state leads to a decline in accountability. Consider the case of the European Commission. No accountant has been able to pass its accounts since the moment of its foundation. And when the accountant draws public attention to this fact, he or she may even be dismissed by the Commissioner supposedly responsible, as someone unfit to hold such an office. The ensuing scandal lasts for a few days, but the Commissioner in question – in the most recent case, Neil Kinnock – simply smiles his way through the storm, confident that nobody is empowered to dismiss him for such a minor bending of the rules. Look at other transnational institutions and you will find that the same kind of corruption prevails. The case of the United Nation (UN) has been well documented: those of the United Nations Educational, Scientific and Cultural Organization (UNESCO), the World Health Organization (WHO) and the International Labour Organization

(ILO) likewise.[16] Nobody is empowered to guard these guardians, since the chain of accountability that allows ordinary citizens to remove them from office has been effectively severed.

Accountability, in short, is a natural by-product of national sovereignty which is jeopardized by transnational governance. The same is true of civil rights. Although the idea of human rights is associated with the Universal Declaration of Human Rights incorporated into the UN Charter, this universalism should be taken with a pinch of salt. Rights do not come into existence merely because they are declared. They come into existence because they can be enforced. They can be enforced only where there is a rule of law. And there is a rule of law only where there is a common obedience, in which the entity enforcing the law is also subject to it. Outside the nation state those conditions have never arisen in modern times.

Societies of citizens enjoy political freedom; but it is not this freedom that guarantees their rights: it is their rights that guarantee their freedom. Rights in turn depend on the web of reciprocal duties, which binds stranger to stranger under a common obedience. That is why the invocation of universal rights – so often made in the name of transnational governance – is so dangerous. Rights are not secured by declaring them. They are secured by the procedures that protect them. And these procedures must be rescued from the State, and from all who would bend them to their own oppressive purposes. That is exactly what our common law jurisdiction has always tried to do. Although the 1689 Bill of Rights declared some of the rights of the British people, it was, in doing so, merely rehearsing established procedures of the common law, and re-affirming them against recent abuses. In particular it upheld the principle contained in the medieval writ of *habeas corpus* – a principle that is not upheld by the *code napoléon* and which is still not enforced in Italy or France, but

---

16   See Rosemary Righter, *Utopia Lost: The United Nations and World Order*, New York: Twentieth Century Fund Press, 1995. On the WHO see Robert D. Tollison and Richard E. Wagner, *Who Benefits from WHO?*, London: Social Affairs Unit, 1993.

which has always been regarded as fundamental in our country, since it places law in the hands of the ordinary person, and removes it from the hands of the State. It is a fundamental link in the chain of accountability, by which our rulers are forced to answer to us for what they do.

The nation state is accountable to all citizens since it owes its existence to the national loyalty that defines its territory and limits its power. When embedded in the law of nation states, therefore, rights become realities; when declared by transnational committees they remain in the realm of dreams – or, if you prefer Bentham's expression, 'nonsense on stilts'.

Panglossian Universalism

The virtues of the nation state do not merely make it the most reliable vehicle for political loyalty in the modern era. They impose upon its critics the obligation to explain just how those virtues could be achieved through transnational government. And this obligation has never been discharged.

The authority habitually cited in defence of transnational government is Kant who, in *Perpetual Peace*, argued for a League of Nations as the way to secure permanent peace in the civilized world.[17] Under the League, sovereign nations would submit to a common jurisdiction, to be enforced by sanctions. The purpose would be to ensure that disputes are settled by law and not by force, with grievances remedied and injustices punished, in the interests of an order beneficial to all. This is the idea embodied first in the League of Nations, which consciously honoured Kant in its name, and then in the United Nations.

What Kant had in mind, however, was very far from transnational government as it is now conceived. He was adamant that there can be no guarantee of peace unless the powers acceding to the treaty are republics. Republican government, as defined by Kant, means representative government under a territorial rule of

---

17 Kant, *Perpetual Peace*, in Hans Reiss (ed.), *Kant: Political Writings* (second edn), Cambridge: CUP, 1991.

law, and although Kant did not emphasize the idea of nationality as its precondition, it is clear from the context that it is self-governing and sovereign nations that he had in mind. Kant went on to argue that the kind of international law that is needed for peace 'presupposes the separate existence of many independent states . . . [united under] a federal union to prevent hostilities breaking out'. This state of affairs is to be preferred to 'an amalgamation of the separate nations under a single power'.[18] And he then gives the principal objection to transnational government, namely that 'laws progressively lose their impact as the government increases its range, and a soulless despotism, after crushing the germs of goodness, will finally lapse into anarchy'.[19]

Kant's *Perpetual Peace* proposed an international jurisdiction with one purpose only – to secure peace between neighbouring jurisdictions. The League of Nations broke down precisely because the background presupposition was not fulfilled – namely, that its members should be republics, in other words states bound together by citizenship. (The rise of totalitarian government in Russia and Germany meant the abolition of citizenship in those countries; and of course it was those countries that were the aggressors in the Second World War.) Kant's presupposition has been cheerfully ignored by the defenders of transnational government, as has the limitation of international jurisdiction to the preservation of peace. We have reached the stage where our national jurisdiction is bombarded by laws from outside – both from the UN and the European Union – even though many of them originate in despotic or criminal governments, and even though hardly any of them are concerned with the maintenance of peace. Even so we, the citizens, are powerless to reject these laws, and they, the legislators, are entirely unanswerable to us, who must obey them. This is exactly what Kant dreaded, as the sure path, first to despotism and then to anarchy. And it is happening. The despotism is coming slowly: the anarchy will happen quickly in its wake, when law is finally detached from the experience of mem-

---

18   *Perpetual Peace, op. cit.*, p. 113.
19   *Ibid.*

bership, becomes 'theirs' but not 'ours' and so loses all authority in the hearts of those whom it presumes to discipline.

The UN Charter of Human Rights and the European Convention of Human Rights belong to the species of utopian thinking that would prefer us to be born into a world without history, without prior attachments, without any of the flesh and blood passions which make government so necessary in the first place. The question never arises, in these documents, of how you persuade people not merely to claim rights, but also to respect them; of how you obtain obedience to a rule of law or a disposition to deal justly and fairly with strangers. Moreover, the judicial bodies established at the Hague and in Strasbourg have been able to extend the list of human rights promiscuously, since they do not have the problem of enforcing them. The burden of transnational legislation falls always on bodies other than those who invent it.

Oikophobia

Nobody brought up in post-war England can fail to be aware of the educated derision that has been directed at our national loyalty by those whose freedom to criticize would have been extinguished years ago, had the English not been prepared to die for their country. The loyalty that people need in their daily lives, and which they affirm in their unconsidered and spontaneous social actions, is now habitually ridiculed or even demonized by the dominant media and the education system. National history is taught as a tale of shame and degradation. The art, literature and music of our nation have been more or less excised from the curriculum, and folkways, local traditions and national ceremonies are routinely rubbished. This repudiation of the national idea is the result of a peculiar frame of mind that has arisen throughout the Western world since the Second World War, and which is particularly prevalent among the intellectual and political elites. No adequate word exists for this attitude, though its symptoms are instantly recognized: namely, the disposition, in any conflict, to side with 'them' against 'us', and the felt need to denigrate the customs, culture and institutions that are identifiably 'ours'. Being the opposite of xenophobia we might describe this state of mind as 'oikophobia', meaning (to stretch the Greek a little) the repudiation of inheritance and home. Oikophobia is a stage through which the adolescent mind normally passes. But it is a stage in which intellectuals tend to become arrested. As George Orwell pointed out, intellectuals on the left are especially prone to it, and this has often made them willing agents of foreign powers.[20] The Cambridge spies offer a telling illustration of what oikophobia has meant for our country. And it is interesting to note that a recent BBC 'docudrama' constructed around that episode neither examined the realities of their treason nor addressed the suffering of the millions of their East European victims, but merely endorsed the oikophobia that had caused the spies to act as they did.

Nor is oikophobia a specifically English, still less specifically British tendency (although Scots seem relatively immune to it). When Sartre and Foucault draw their picture of the 'bourgeois' mentality, the mentality of the Other in his Otherness, they are describing the ordinary decent Frenchman, and expressing their contempt for his national culture. A chronic form of oikophobia has spread through the American universities, in the guise of political correctness, and loudly surfaced in the aftermath of September 11, to pour scorn on the culture that allegedly provoked the attacks, and to side by implication with the terrorists.

The domination of our own national parliament by oikophobes is partly responsible for the assaults on our constitution, for the acceptance of subsidized immigration and for the attacks on customs and institutions associated with traditional and native forms of life. The oikophobe repudiates national loyalties and defines his goals and ideals *against* the nation, promoting transnational institutions over national governments, accepting and endorsing laws that are imposed on us from on high by the EU or the UN, though without troubling to consider Terence's question, and defining his political vision in terms of universal values that have been purified of all reference to the particular attachments of

---

20   *The Lion and the Unicorn*, London: Secker & Warburg, 1941.

a real historical community. The oikophobe is, in his own eyes, a defender of enlightened universalism against local chauvinism. And it is the rise of the oikophobe that has led to the growing crisis of legitimacy in the nation states of Europe. For we are seeing a massive expansion of the legislative burden on the people of Europe, and a relentless assault on the only loyalties that would enable them voluntarily to bear it. The explosive effect of this has already been felt in Holland and France. It may be felt everywhere soon, and the result may not be what the oikophobes expect.

Threats to the Nation

I am not alone in believing that the greatest political decisions now confronting us concern the nation and its future. These decisions must be discussed with the utmost honesty if we are to do what is best for our country and for the world. Honesty is difficult, however, since censorship prevails in the media and in the circles of government. Those who defend the first-person plural of nationhood, in however nuanced a way and with however mild a tongue, are apt to be branded as fascists, racists, xenophobes, nostalgists or at best (in our case) Little Englanders. Their arguments are habitually drowned under platitudes about the multicultural society, the rights of minorities and the new global economy. Powerful bureaucracies in the EU, the UN and the World Trade Organization amplify the calls for a new world order, and cast further scorn on the reactionaries who impede their plans. In the emerging conditions it is only the United States of America that actively resists the expropriation of its sovereignty by the UN, and it is little short of a paradox that a state formed by federation, constitution and conscious political choice should now be the strongest defender of national sovereignty. Why that is so is a difficult question to answer. But it is so, and it is one explanation of the growing divergence of the American and the European vision of government.[21] Moreover, American resistance to the legislative powers of the UN, which threatens its sov-

---

21   But see Robert Kagan, *Of Paradise and Power*, New York: Knopf, 2003.

ereignty, should be set beside its acquiescence in, and indeed exploitation of, the legislative powers of the WTO, which threatens the sovereignty of everyone else. I return to this point below, since it represents the great blind spot in American policy-making in this area.

Those who come to the West in search of citizenship include many who respond to the gift of it with gratitude and loyalty. This is especially true of those who battle against hardship in order to reach our shores, who work to establish themselves and who take the entire risk of their migration upon themselves. Unfortunately, such immigrants are now untypical. Asylum seekers enjoy a subsidized existence from the moment of their arrival, the government being obliged by the UN Convention on Refugees and Asylum to offer hospitality at the citizens' expense. The stock of social housing, which represents the savings of local communities, built up on the understanding that this housing was for the use of those who already belong and to whom we owe a neighbourly duty, has been commandeered by incomers who are not neighbours at all. The impact of this on sentiments of national loyalty is little short of catastrophic.

Quite suddenly what was *ours* becomes *theirs*, and the discovery that there is nothing to be done to remedy the situation, that no law, court or government can be appealed to and that the expropriation cannot therefore be peacefully ended, has a profound impact on people's sense of identity. An identity forged from a shared sense of home is by its very nature threatened by the person who comes to the home uninvited, and with a non-negotiable demand for sanctuary. You may not approve of that fact, but it is a fact nevertheless, and the principal cost of national loyalties. And if it is a cost that you feel cannot be borne, try loyalties of another kind – ethnic, for example, as in the Balkans, or religious, as in the Middle East. In any case, there is no denying that, as a result of the asylum crisis, a gap has opened up between government and people: the 'we' feeling seems no longer to have a voice among our rulers, and – at the same time as making urgent appeals to *us* for patience, tolerance and good will towards strangers – the Government continues to act not on *our* behalf but *theirs*.

It is important to see that this national crisis is the direct result of transnational legislation, and could be solved at once were our political leaders to put the national interest before the artificial obligations imposed by the UN and the EU. The UN Convention on Refugees and Asylum dates from 1951, when there were hardly any refugees or asylum seekers in the world. But it has bound the legislatures of the nation states ever since, despite radically changed circumstances. The Convention enables dictators to export their opponents without earning the bad name that comes from killing them. The entire cost of the Convention is therefore borne by the law-abiding states – in other words the nation states – whose legal and fiscal systems are now under intolerable strain as a result of the influx of refugees. Delicate matters over which our legislators and judiciary have expended decades of careful reflection (planning law, for example) with the all-important aim of sustaining national loyalty by reconciling *us* with *our neighbours* are thrown into disarray by a measure that is imposed on us by a bureaucratic system that we can only pretend to control.

An uneasy silence, induced by self-censorship and intimidation, has so far prevailed concerning this, the most important issue facing modern Europe. But people are beginning to wake up to the effect of unwanted immigration not merely on national loyalty, but on the idea of citizenship which has until now been taken for granted. It is now possible to claim the benefits of citizenship, to sue for them as 'human rights' and to acknowledge no duty to the State in return. Asylum seekers can even claim welfare benefits and sue local councils that do not provide accommodation, while at the same time preparing *jihad* against their hosts – a spectacle that has profoundly shocked native British citizens, and which recalls the situation dramatized by Max Frisch in *The Fire Raisers*. The idea that the citizen owes loyalty to a country, a territory, a jurisdiction and all those who reside within it – the root assumption of democratic politics, and one that depends upon the nation as its moral foundation – that idea has no place in the minds and hearts of many who now call themselves citizens of European states.

The external threat to national sovereignty is familiar from debates over the EU and the UN. But these are not the only attempts to expropriate legislative powers from national parliaments and to vest them in unaccountable bureacracies. There is also the World Trade Organization – the blind spot in the American strategy for a world of sovereign democracies. The WTO has undeniably enhanced the volume of world trade. And this has benefited the economies of some poor countries – at least, in so far as benefit is measured in terms of GDP. But the WTO process has been conducted without regard for the identity of those who are compelled by economic *force majeure* to take part in it. It has now reached the point where delegates can argue – on behalf of multinational businesses like Monsanto – that national sovereignty is a 'block on free trade', and that corporations should be able to sue national governments if they have been denied 'investor rights', as when a national government gives preferential terms to native firms.[22] In effect, the WTO is going the way of the EU. By pursuing free trade at all costs, it threatens the thing that makes international trade into a durable and beneficial feature of the human condition – namely, national sovereignty.

The result of the WTO's assault on national jurisdictions is apparent everywhere: in the destruction of local food economies by multinational agribusiness; in the overriding of local property laws and barriers to migration; in the increasing ownership of land by people who have no obligation to defend it against invasion; in the control of vital services in one country by people who are citizens of another. And so on. In short, multinational businesses have used the transnational institutions in the same

---

22 Such were the provisions of the proposed Multinational Agreeement on Investment, which was not in fact adopted by the WTO, following a campaign against it, but whose provisions are constantly being resurrected by multinationals at the WTO negotiations. Moreover, some of these provisions are already incorporated into the North American Free Trade Agreement under Chapter 11, effectively neutralizing attempts by the Canadian government to protect its sovereignty in matters vital to its survival. Thus the government of British Columbia is currently being sued by a US water corporation for having banned the export of its water. See Paul Kingsnorth, 'Cancun: Why You Should Care', in *The Ecologist*, June 2003.

way as the oikophobes – to break down national jurisdictions and to cancel the loyalties on which they depend. The incongruous alliance of the spivs and the oiks will spell the doom of both; but the result will not be a happy one for the rest of us.

A national parliament is accountable to the people who elected it, and must serve their interests. It must strive to reconcile the competing claims that come before it, to balance one claim against another, and to achieve a solution that will enable people to live in harmony as neighbours. A transnational assembly need obey – and can obey – no such constraints. Normally, it has just one legislative goal – in the case of the WTO the advancement of free trade – and no duty to reconcile that goal with all the other goods and needs of a real human society. That is why its rulings are so dangerous. They are made on the strength of reasoning that ignores the real database from which rational political choices must be made. The UN Convention on Asylum and Refugees was proposed as an answer to one problem only – and a problem whose scale and gravity have since immeasurably increased. The UN Assembly had no duty to reconcile its ruling with the many interests that will inevitably conflict with it, and no duty to return to the matter when conditions have changed. The ruling is therefore irrational, in the true sense of ignoring almost all the data that are relevant to its justification. Exactly the same criticism should be made of every single decision made by the WTO – even those which seem advantageous to everyone.

Overcoming the Threats

The threats to national loyalty are serious and disturbing. But I do not think that we are powerless in the face of them. The external threat comes from political weakness. A concerted effort to return from transnational legislation to bilateral agreements would restore much of our lost sovereignty. Since the institutions pressing us to accept their legislative prescriptions – the UN, the WTO, the EU – are without any effective military arm the cost of defying them will be rapidly outweighed by the benefit. And the cost of obeying them will be a complete disappearance of national loyalty. But they in turn are parasitic on national loyalty and could not survive without it. Hence, whether we obey them or defy them, these transnational organizations are destined to disappear.

The problem posed by the global economy and the outreach of the multinationals can be solved in a similar spirit. It is only free-market dogma that persuades people that free trade is a real possibility in the modern world. All trade is massively subsidized, usually in the interests of the stronger party – as American agriculture is subsidized, not merely by direct payments to farmers but by laws that permit crops ruled unsafe elsewhere, by standards in animal welfare that we in Britain would not countenance, by the existence of publicly funded roads and infrastructure that ensure rapid transport of goods to the port of exit, and so on. And all trade is or ought to be subject to prohibition and restriction in the interest not merely of local conditions but also of moral, religious and national imperatives. If free trade means the importation of pornography into Islamic countries, who can defend it? If it means taking advantage of sweated or even slave labour where that is available and importing the tortured remains of battery-farmed animals wherever they can be sold, why is it such a boon? If it means allowing anonymous shareholders who neither know nor care about Hungary to own and control the Budapest water supply, is it not the most dangerous of long-term policies? The fact is that free trade is neither possible nor desirable. It is for each nation to establish the regulatory regime that will maximize trade with its neighbours, while protecting the local customs, moral ideals and privileged relations on which national identity depends.

The internal threats to nationality are more difficult to confront. But again the matter is not hopeless. Immigration controls have collapsed largely as a result of transnational legislation. Restore sovereignty and these controls can be once again put in place. Return control of the education system to parents and the oikophobes will no longer be in charge of it. Withdraw from the European Convention on Human Rights and historical allegiance can once again regulate relations between the citizens of European states, with duties re-affirmed as the enduring price of their rights. All those are feasible policies and indeed have been, in various combinations, proposed by democratic parties contending for power in the national parliaments of Europe.

Those who excuse the bureaucratic excesses of the EU often argue that we must be part of the Union, in order to influence it. And by arguing in that way they show their deep agreement with what I have tried to put across in this chapter. They too recognize that the question of the EU is a question of our destiny, our decisions, our autonomy, our long-term interests. And that 'our' is defined over the territory of a nation state. The accession states of Eastern Europe are joining the Union, not in order to renounce their sovereignty, but in order to protect it from the threats posed until now by the Russian behemoth and in order to shorten the painful transition to a full capitalist economy. Turkey longs to join the EU in order to ratify its status as a nation state, and to protect its nationhood from the religious and tribal loyalties that threaten it from the south and the east. In short, the EU depends upon the thing that it seems bent on destroying. By restoring sovereignty to our national parliaments, we would therefore bring hope to our continent. By removing sovereignty from them, we shall invite first the despotism and then the anarchy that Kant feared.

2
Conserving Nature

Environmentalism has recently tended to recruit from people on the left, offering ecological rectitude as part of a comprehensive call for 'social justice'. However, concern for the environment is shared by people of quite the opposite temperament, for whom constitutions and procedures are more important than social goals, and who regard the egalitarian project with scepticism. The appropriation of the environmental movement by the left is in fact a relatively new phenomenon. In Britain the movement has its roots in the nineteenth-century reaction to the Industrial Revolution, in which Tories and radicals played an equal part, and the early opposition to industrial farming joins guild socialists like H. J. Massingham, Tories like Lady Eve Balfour and eccentric radicals like Rolf Gardiner, who borrowed ideas from left and right and who has even been identified (by Patrick Wright) as a kind of fascist.[23] Moreover, contemporary environmentalists are aware of the ecological damage done by revolutionary socialism – as in the forced collectivization, frenzied industrialization and gargantuan plans to shift populations, rivers and whole landscapes that we have witnessed in the Soviet Union and China. Left-wing thinkers will not regard those abuses as the inevitable result of their ideas. Nevertheless, they will recognize that more work is needed, if the normal conscience is to be persuaded that socialism contains the answer to the growing ecological problem.

---

23   See Patrick Wright, 'An Encroachment Too Far', in Anthony Barnett and Roger Scruton (eds), *Town and Country*, London: Jonathan Cape, 1998.

At the same time, they seldom recognize any affinity with 'the right', and often seem to regard 'conservatism' as a dirty word, with no semantic connection to the 'conservation' that they favour.

The explanation, I believe, is that environmentalists have been habituated to see conservatism as the ideology of free enterprise, and free enterprise as an assault on the Earth's resources, with no motive beyond the short-term gains that animate the market. Those who have called themselves conservatives in the political context are in part responsible for this misperception. For they have tended to see modern politics in terms of a simple dichotomy between individual freedom on the one hand and state control on the other. Individual freedom means economic freedom and this, in turn, means the freedom to exploit natural resources for financial gain. The timber merchant who cuts down a rain forest, the mining corporation that ransacks the subsoil, the motor manufacturer who churns out an unending stream of cars, the cola merchant who sends out a million plastic bottles each day – all are obeying the laws of the market, and all, unless checked, are destroying some part of our collective environment. And because in a market economy the biggest actors do the most damage, environmentalists turn their hostility on big businesses, and on the free economies that produce them.

Abolish the market economy, however, and the normal result is enterprises that are just as large and just as destructive but which, because they are in the hands of the State, are usually answerable to no sovereign power that can limit their predations. It is a plausible conservative response, therefore, not to advocate economic freedom at all costs, but to recognize the costs of economic freedom and to take all steps to reduce them. We need free enterprise, but we also need the rule of law that limits it. When enterprise is the prerogative of the State, the entity that controls the law is identical with the entity that has the most powerful motive to evade it – a sufficient explanation, it seems to me, of the ecological catastrophe of socialist economies.

However, there is another and better reason for thinking that conservatism and environmentalism are natural bedfellows. As I argued in the Introduction to this book, conservatism is an exercise in social ecology. Individual freedom is a part of that ecology, since without it social organisms cannot adapt. But freedom is not the sole or even the central goal of politics, even if it is the attribute that, at a deep level, makes politics both necessary and possible. Conservatism and conservation are in fact two aspects of a single long-term policy, which is that of husbanding resources. These resources include the social capital embodied in laws, customs and institutions; they also include the material capital contained in the environment, and the economic capital contained in a free, but law-governed, economy. The purpose of politics, on this view, is not to rearrange society in the interests of some overarching vision or ideal, such as equality, liberty or fraternity. It is to maintain a vigilant resistance to the entropic forces that erode our social and ecological inheritance. The goal is to pass on to future generations – and if possible to enhance – the order and equilibrium of which we are the temporary trustees.

The conservative understanding of political action is therefore formulated, as a rule, in terms of trusteeship rather than enterprise, of conversation rather than command, of friendship rather than solidarity.[24] Those ideas lend themselves readily to the environmental project, and it always surprises me that so few environmentalists seem to see this. It is obvious to a conservative that our reckless pursuit of individual gratification jeopardizes the social order just as it jeopardizes the planet. And it is obvious too that the wisest policies are those that strive to protect and keep in place the institutions that place a brake on our appetites, and which renew the sources of social contentment.

The major difficulty, from the environmental point of view, is that social equilibrium and ecological equilibrium are not the same idea, and not necessarily in harmony. Two examples illustrate the problem. Democracies seem to achieve equilibrium only

---

24   Trusteeship is associated with Burke, Moser and Gierke; conversation with Oakeshott; friendship with Aristotle. All are trying to reconstruct political authority as something intrinsically welcome to those who are subject to it.

in a condition of economic growth. Periods of stagnation, rapid inflation or impoverishment are also periods of radical discontent, in which envy, resentment and anger lead to instability. Hence the first concern of democratic governments is to encourage economic growth, regardless of the environmental costs of it. We see this in the present British Government's attitude to airports, business parks and roads, the environmental impact of which is put out of mind, once these things are seen as economic assets. We see it, too, in the American response to the Kyoto accords. It is not big business that puts the real pressure on the American House of Representatives not to ratify such agreements, but the desire of its members to be re-elected.

Nor is democracy the only problematic case. Other forms of social equilibrium may equally pose a threat to the environment, not because they depend on economic growth, but because they depend on population growth, or on the consumption of some finite resource like a rain forest. The conservative response to this kind of problem is to recognize that environmental equilibirium is a part of any durable social order. The conception put before us by Burke is in fact one that ought to appeal to environmentalists. Burke's response to Rousseau's theory of the social contract was to acknowledge that political order is like a contract, but to add that it is not a contract between the living only, but between the living, the unborn and the dead.[25] In other words, to speak plainly, not a contract at all, but a relation of trusteeship, in which inherited benefits are conserved and passed on. The living may have an interest in consuming the Earth's resources, but it was not for this that the dead laboured. And the unborn depend upon our restraint. Long-term social equilibrium, therefore, must include ecological equilibrium.

This thesis, which environmentalists are apt to express in terms of 'sustainability', is better expressed in Burke's way. For Burke reminds us of a motive that arises naturally in human beings, and which can be exploited for the wider purpose of environmental and institutional conservation: namely, love. This motive leads

---

25 *Reflections on the Revolution in France*, London, 1790.

people both to create good things and to destroy them. But it turns of its own accord in a direction that favours conservation, since human love extends to the dead and the unborn: we mourn the one and plan for the other out of a natural superfluity of good will. True social equilibrium arises when the institutions are in place that encourage that superfluity and channel it towards the maintenance of the social organism. The principal danger is that those institutions might be destroyed in the name of present emergencies, present appetites and the egregious needs of the merely living.

This emphasis on small-scale, observable and believable human motives is one of the strong points of conservative political thinking. Socialists place before us ideals of equality and social justice. But they seldom trouble to ask whether anyone – still less whether everyone – is motivated to pursue those things. The same problem arises with the environmentalists' goal of sustainability. It may be my goal and yours: but what about Jill, John and Marianne? Liberals are on safer ground with their ruling concept of liberty: it can be assumed that rational beings will aim for liberty, since liberty is the precondition of aiming for anything. On the other hand, my liberty may be your servitude; the pursuit of liberty does not guarantee that liberty will be available to all. And while it is true that people often surrender part of their liberty, the principle cause of their doing so is the emotion – namely, love – that conservatives wish to place at the heart of the social organism.

It seems to me that the greatest weakness in radical environmentalism has been its failure to explore the question of human motivation. There is one overwhelming reason for the degradation of the environment, and that is human appetite. In the wealthier parts of the world people are too many, too mobile, too eager to gratify their every desire, too unconcerned about the waste that builds up in their wake, too ready, in the jargon of economics, to externalize their costs. Most of our environmental problems are special cases of this general problem. And the problem can be more simply described as the triumph of desire over restraint. It can be solved only when restraint prevails over desire, in other words, only when people have re-learned the habit of sacrifice. For what do people make sacrifices? For the things that they love. And when do these sacrifices benefit the unborn? When they are made for the dead. Such was the core sentiment to which Burke and de Maistre made appeal.

There is a tendency on the left to single out the big players in the market as the principal culprits: to pin environmental crime on those – like oil companies, motor manufacturers, logging corporations, agribusinesses, supermarkets – who make their profits by exporting their costs to future generations. But this is to mistake the effect for the cause. In a free market these ways of making money emerge by an invisible hand from choices made by all of us. It is the demand for cars, oil, cheap food and expendable luxuries that is the real cause of the industries that provide these things. Of course it is true that the big players externalize their costs whenever they can. But so do we. Whenever we travel by air, whenever we visit the supermarket, whenever we consume fossil fuels, we are exporting our costs to future generations. A free economy is one that is driven by individual demand. The solution is not the socialist one, of abolishing the free economy, since this merely places massive economic power in the hands of unaccountable bureaucrats, who are equally in the business of exporting their costs. The solution is to rectify our demands, so as to bear the costs of them ourselves. In short, we must change our lives. And we can change our lives only if we have a motive to do so – a motive that is strong enough to constrain our appetites.

When Burke invoked our feelings towards the dead he was placing in the centre of political order a universal emotion which, he believed, could safeguard the long-term interests of society. But this motive extends no further than our local and contingent attachments. Through institutions of membership and the 'little platoons' that shape our allegiances we can extend our social concern beyond our immediate family. Nevertheless, the sense of a shared inheritance does not extend to all mankind, and the respect for the dead – which is a respect for *our* dead, for those who have made sacrifices on *our* behalf – peters out at the social horizon, where 'we' shades into 'they'.[26] Modern societies are societies of strangers. And one of the underlying conservative projects in our times has been to discover the kind of affection that can bind such a society together across generations, without risking fragmentation along family, tribal or mafia lines. Hence the importance in conservative thinking of the nation and the nation state, as I described them in the last chapter.

Conservatives are not in the business of conserving just any law, institution or custom. Their desire is to conserve the institutions that embody collective solutions to recurring problems, and which pass on socially generated knowledge. In Burke's view (and mine) the common law is such an institution; so are political institutions like representative government, and social institutions like marriage and the family. These are institutions that foster the habit of sacrifice, and which therefore generate the motive on which the husbanding of resources depends.

Now there is a real cost involved in upholding such institutions and defending them from predation – a cost that imbues Burke's *Reflections on the French Revolution* with its air of solemn melancholy. For entropy can beset even the most settled form of human engagement. The social conservative who, for example, defends the family in modern conditions attracts the anger of those who have liberated themselves from this particular institutional constraint. It does no good to follow Charles Murray and James Q. Wilson in pointing out the social costs of single-parenthood and divorce.[27] For that is simply to speak for future generations, people who don't yet exist, and who have been dropped from the equation.

Something similar happens when we consider questions of ecology. To defend slow food, slow transport and low energy con-

---

26   This theme is beginning to enter the environmental literature, thanks to writers like Avner de-Shalit (*Why Posterity Matters*, London: Routledge, 1998) and John O'Neill (*Ecology, Policy and Politics*, Cambridge: CUP, 2001).

27   Charles Murray, *Losing Ground: American Social Policy 1950–1980*, New York: Basic Books, 1984; James Q. Wilson, *The Moral Sense*, New York: The Free Press, 1993.

sumption in a society addicted to fast food, tourism, luxury and waste is to risk the anger of those who need to be converted. Not only are there no votes to be won by seeking to close airports, to narrow roads or to return to a local food economy, there is the serious risk of making matters worse, by representing environmental protection as the cause of nostalgic cranks. All environmental activists are familiar with this reaction. But I am surprised that they do not see that it is a version of the very same reaction that is directed towards social conservatives, when they defend the beleaguered moral order that was – until a few decades ago – passed from generation to generation as a matter of course. Environmentalists and conservatives are both in search of the motive that will defend a shared but threatened legacy from predation by its current trustees.

Rational self-interest is not, I think, the motive that we are seeking. For rational self-interest is subject to the well-known free-rider and prisoner's dilemma syndromes, and cannot avert, but on the contrary will always promote, 'the tragedy of the commons'.[28] Social contract theorists, from Hobbes to Rawls, have attempted to overcome this problem, but always they come up against some version of the original difficulty: why is it more reasonable to bide by the contract than to pretend to bide by it?

What is needed is a non-egotistic motive that can be elicited in ordinary members of society, and relied upon to serve the long-term ecological goal. Burke proposed 'the hereditary principle', as protecting important institutions from pillage or decay, and believed that people have a natural tendency to accept the limits that this principle places on their desires. Hegel argued for the priority of non-contractual obligations, of the kind that sustain the family, and believed that similar obligations could be recuperated and exercised at the political level. In similar vein, de Maistre gave a central place to piety, as a motive that puts divinely ordained traditions and constitutions above the temptations of self-interest.

---

28 Garrett Hardin, 'The Tragedy of the Commons', *Science* 162: 1, 243–8, 1968.

None of those suggestions is likely to carry complete conviction today, though each tries to frame a picture of human motivation that does not make rational self-interest the sole ground for collective decision-making. Burke's invocation of the hereditary principle is of particular interest, however, since it engages directly with what he predicted (rightly as it happened) would be the outcome of the French Revolution – namely a squandering of inherited resources and a wholesale loss of what is now called 'social capital', including law, educational institutions and public or quasi-public endowments.

Burke's model of inheritance was the English hereditary estate, which removed assets from the market, protected them from pillage and erected in the place of absolute ownership a kind of trusteeship, with the life-tenant as beneficiary. This institution, protected by law, withheld land and natural resources from exploitation, and endowed tenants for life with a kind of sovereignty on condition that they passed the land unencumbered to their heirs. No environmentalist can be insensible of the enormous ecological benefit of 'settled land', so conceived. This was a resource that could not be exploited for all it was worth. It had to be used for the benefit of the 'successors in title' – in other words, sustainably. Modern environmentalists are likely to be sensible, too, of the social inequalities and hierarchies that this form of ownership perpetuated. And those of a leftist persuasion will no doubt share the passionate distaste expressed by Raymond Williams for a social order that (according to Williams at least) kept the real producers unrewarded and the idlers forever in clover.[29] The Settled Land Acts, passed and amended at various times during the nineteenth and early-twentieth centuries, gave tenants for life the right to convert landed estates into monetary capital, by selling the land to someone who would be free to develop it and retaining the proceeds in trust for the successors in title. In no time the industrialists and the mining corporations had moved in. The result was a vast increase in the

---

29   Raymond Williams, *The Country and the City*, London: Fontana, 1975.

wealth of Britain, the first steps towards social equality and a century of environmental destruction.

Burke saw the hereditary principle as a psychological obstacle before those who had wished to lay their hands on the estates, the endowments, the church-owned and institution-owned buildings and treasuries that had safeguarded the national assets of France from generation to generation. And he foresaw that, once the principle was rejected, restraint would have no motive, and the assets would be seized and squandered. But to respect the hereditary principle means to accept unequal holdings, hereditary status and the influence of family over individual fortunes. It is impossible to combine this state of mind with the modern demand for equality, which loudly affirms the rights of the living over the paper claims of the dead.

We cannot return to the kind of social motivations that Burke called upon: people don't think that way any more. But we should take a lesson from Burke, Hegel and de Maistre. We should recognize that environmental protection is a lost cause if we cannot find the human motive that would lead people in general, and not merely their self-appointed representatives, to advance it. And here, I think, is where environmentalists and conservatives can and should make common cause. And that common cause is local – specifically national – loyalty.

Many environmentalists on the left will acknowledge that local loyalties and local concerns must be given a proper place in our decision-making, if we are to counter the adverse effects of the global economy. But they will tend to baulk at the suggestion that local loyalty should be seen in national, rather than communitarian, terms. However, there is a very good reason for emphasizing nationality. For nations are communities with a political shape. They are predisposed to assert their sovereignty, by translating the common sentiment of belonging into collective decisions and self-imposed laws. Nationality is a form of territorial attachment. But it is also a proto-legislative arrangement. And it is through developing this idea, of a territorial sentiment that contains the seeds of sovereignty within itself, that conservatives make their distinctive contribution to ecological thinking.

A useful contrast is provided by George Monbiot, who has trenchantly argued the case for some kind of global politics, through which ordinary people can fend off the disasters that are being concocted within the global economy, and give voice to their desire for a safe, equitable and sustainable economic order.[30] And I suspect that this would be the preferred way forward for those who have retained some vestige of the old socialist agenda, and who still wish to combine environmental rectitude with social justice. However, this approach is premised on two highly questionable assumptions: first that sustainability and social justice can be combined, and second that ordinary people, given the choice, would opt for sustainability rather than instant gratification. In some circumstances they would, of course. But it is precisely those circumstances that the global economy destroys.

The conservative approach, it seems to me, is more reasonable, even if it is also less ambitious. Rather than attempt to rectify environmental and social problems on the global level, conservatives seek local controls and a reassertion of local sovereignty over known and managed environments. This means affirming the right of nations to self-government, and to the adoption of policies that will chime with local loyalties and sentiments of national pride. The attachment to territory and the desire to protect that territory from erosion and waste remain powerful motives, and ones that are presupposed in all demands for sacrifice that issue from the mouths of politicians. For this motive is the simple and powerful one, of love for one's home.

It is only at this local level that I believe it is realistic to hope for improvement. For there is no evidence that global political institutions have done anything to limit the global entropy. On the contrary, by encouraging communication around the world and by eroding national sovereignty and legislative barriers, they have fed into that global entropy and weakened the only true sources of resistance to it. I know many environmentalists who seem to agree with me that the WTO is now a threat to the environment, not merely by breaking down self-sufficient and self-reproducing

---

30   *The Age of Consent*, London: Penguin, 2002.

peasant economies, but also by eroding national sovereignty wherever this places an obstacle before the goals of multinational investors. And many seem to agree with me that traditional communities deserve protection from sudden and externally engineered change, not merely for the sake of their sustainable economies, but also because of the values and loyalties that constitute the sum of their social capital. The odd thing is that so few environmentalists follow the logic of this argument to its conclusion, and recognize that we too deserve protection from global entropy; that we too must retain national sovereignty as our greatest political asset in the face of it; and that we too must retain what we can of the loyalties that attach us to our territory, and make of that territory a home. Yet, in so far as we have seen any successful attempts to reverse the tide of ecological destruction, these have issued from national or local schemes, to protect territory recognized as 'ours' – defined, in other words, through some inherited entitlement. I am thinking of the recycling initiatives that are gradually freeing Germany from the plague of plastic bottles, the legislation that freed certain states of the United States from polythene bags, the clean-energy initiatives in Sweden and Norway, the Swiss planning laws that have enabled local communities to retain control over their environments and to think of those environments as a shared possession, and so on. These are small-scale achievements, but they are better than nothing. Moreover, they are successful because they make appeal to a natural motive – which is love of country, love of territory and love of that territory as home.

That, it seems to me, is the goal towards which serious environmentalism and serious conservatism both point – namely, home, the place where we are, the place that defines us, that we hold in trust for our descendants and that we don't want to spoil. Many of those who have seen this connection between conservatism and environmentalism have also – like Patrick Wright – been suspicious of it.[31] And local environmentalism between the wars – especially in Germany – was undeniably part of the

---

31   See 'An Encroachment Too Far', *op. cit.*

collectivist frame of mind, even if only circumstantially connected to the Nazi and Communist frenzy. However, I think it is time to take a more open-minded and imaginative vision of what conservatism and environmentalism have to offer each other. For nobody seems to have identified a motive more likely to serve the environmentalist cause than this one, of the shared love for our home. It is a motive in ordinary people. It can provide a foundation both for a conservative approach to institutions and a conservationist approach to the land. It is a motive that might permit us to reconcile the demand for democratic participation with the respect for absent generations and the duty of trusteeship. It is, in my view, the only serious recourse that we have, in our fight to maintain local order in the face of globally stimulated decay. And it is worth adding that, in so far as thermodynamics has a story to tell, it is this one.

This is why I think conservatives are likely to dissociate themselves from currently fashionable forms of environmental activism. Radical environmentalists are heirs to the leftist suspicion of nations and nationhood. They repudiate old hierarchies, and strive to remove the dead from their agenda, being largely unmoved by Burke's thought that, in doing so, they also remove the unborn. They define their goals in global and international terms, and support NGOs and pressure groups which they believe will fight the multinational predators on their own territory and with weapons that make no use of national sovereignty.

Conservatives dislike this approach for two reasons. First, the NGOs and pressure groups that are favoured by the activists are as unaccountable and unrepresentative as the predators they oppose. Second, they recruit their following through hatred and demonization – hatred of the big businesses, the big polluters, the apologists for capitalism and so on, against whom they see themselves pitted as David against Goliath. In other words, they put politics on a war footing, in the manner of St Just and Lenin. This runs totally counter to the conservative desire to found politics in friendship and conversation, and to resolve conflicts wherever possible through dialogue. Conservatives tend to see the environmental NGOs, like Greenpeace, as threats to social equilibrium, on account of their desire to pin on the big actors blame which should in fact be distributed across us all. And by casting the conflict in the form of a zero-sum game between themselves and the enemy, they obscure what it is really about, which is the accountability of both.

The point can be illustrated in the remarkable case of Greenpeace versus Shell, over the matter of the Brent Spar oil rig, which Shell had proposed to dispose of by sinking it in the sea. Greenpeace weighed in with a massively orchestrated hate campaign against Shell, involving boycotts, advertising, leaflets and pressure on shareholders, in order to prevent the sinking of the oil rig. The reason given was that the rig contained many thousand tonnes of oil and would be an environmental hazard for years to come: a reason that turned out to be false. No suggestion was made that Greenpeace and Shell should sit down together and discuss the problem. This was a fight to the death, between the forces of light and the forces of darkness. Greenpeace won and the rig is now rusting in a Norwegian fjord, an unsightly wreck costing many millions to dismantle, a process that will certainly be far more polluting than the one originally proposed by the corporation. Having cost Shell millions of dollars and unjustly damaged its reputation, Greenpeace, on proof that the rig after all contained no oil, offered an airy apology and went on to its next campaign.

In such examples we see how environmental activism, divorced from national sentiments that can carry the people with it, and expressed through unaccountable bodies that follow self-chosen global agendas, does little or nothing to further the environmental cause. And conservatives will see this as an inevitable result of the radical mindset. Radicals prefer global ideals to local loyalties, and rather than making bridges to their opponents, prefer to demonize them (as Bjørn Lomborg, for example, has been demonized in recent assaults on his work). Institutions like Greenpeace bypass national governments, while exerting force that need never account for its misuse. They exhibit the exultant self-righteousness that Burke discerned in the French Revolution, and which he believed would lead not merely to the disenfranchizing of ordinary citizens, but to the squandering of their inheritance.

My own hope is that environmentalists will grow out of the witch-hunting mentality that has alienated conservatives, and that conservatives will cease to be defensive about their true agenda, which is the one implied in their name. I would like to see an *Ecologist* magazine that makes room, in its scheme of things, for old Tory values of loyalty and allegiance. For it seems to me that the dominance of international decision-making by unaccountable bureaucracies, unaccountable NGOs and corporations accountable only to their shareholders (who may have no attachment to the environment which the corporations threaten) has made it more than ever necessary for us to follow the conservative path. We need to retreat from the global back to the local, so as to address the problems that we can collectively identify as ours, with means that we can control, from motives that we all feel. And that means being clear as to who *we* are, and why we are in it together and committed to our common survival. I respect George Monbiot's attempt to identify this first-person plural in planetary terms, just as I respect the Enlightenment conception of the human being as a rational agent motivated by universal principles. As a conservative, however, I bow to the evidence of history, which tells me that human beings are creatures of limited and local affections, the best of which is the territorial loyalty that leads them to live at peace with strangers, to honour their dead and to make provision for those who will one day replace them in their earthly tenancy.

3

Eating our Friends

The consensus among the monotheistic religions has been that animals exist for our purposes and that we are entitled to use them, domesticate them and eat them, subject only to God's inscrutable dietary laws. Like much else that was once the prerogative of religion, the treatment of animals has now become a matter of ordinary morality, with no shortage of sermons directed at the hunters, fur-wearers and carnivores from the puritans who cannot abide the sight of sinful pleasure. The conflict over eating animals has indeed become a test case for moral theory in Western societies, not least because of the vigorous campaigns conducted by Peter Singer, the Australian philosopher who has applied an uncompromising utilitarianism to the problem, concluding not merely that much that we do to animals cannot be defended but that our entire common-sense morality, which elevates human beings above other animals, is founded on a mistake.[32] In confronting the opponents of hunting, fur-wearing and meat-eating, therefore, we soon find ourselves exploring the grounds of moral judgements, and the nature of the beings who make them.

The moral life, I believe, rests on three pillars: value, virtue and duty.[33] Some believe that all the weight can be made to rest on only one of those: value, in the case of most utilitarians, duty in

---

32 Peter Singer, *Animal Liberation*, Oxford: OUP, 1975.
33 This is the view that I have defended, in specific reference to our treatment of animals, in *Animal Rights and Wrongs* (third edn), London: Metro Books, 2000.

the case of their deontological opponents. Advocates of virtue ethics, like Rosalind Hursthouse, ask us to see the legalistic side of morality (the 'moral code') as part of virtue.[34] I am not sure that any of these reductions can be successfully carried out or that they need to be carried out. But I am sure that we cannot give a coherent account of the moral life, if we do not do justice to all the conceptions that support it – to value, virtue and duty – and if we do not show their place in the good life for a human being.

There is another aspect of human nature, left out of account by all the standard treatments of ethics, which I have a strong urge also to place at the very centre of the subject, and especially when the subject is our relation to the natural world: namely piety, by which I mean a certain disposition to acknowledge our weak and dependent state, and to face the surrounding world with due reverence and humility. This feeling is the residue of religion in all of us, whether or not we wish to admit it. It is the attitude that so many people – environmentalists, conservationists and animal welfare activists included – are attempting to re-capture, in a world where the results of human presumption are so depressingly apparent. Even in an age that does not recognize it under its traditional name, piety is ever-present, a necessary motive in the living and a guarantee offered to those unborn. I suspect that the deepest motive for vegetarianism is the sense of the impious nature of much that we do by way of supplying, fulfilling and displaying our appetite for the flesh of other species.

Unlike the other animals with which we come into regular contact, we are self-conscious, our thoughts involve 'I'-thoughts, 'you'-thoughts and 'he, she, we and they'-thoughts. Because of language, and the intellectual structure that language makes available, we do not live, like other animals, in a 'world of perception', to use Schopenhauer's phrase. Our thoughts and feelings range over the actual and the possible, the probable and the necessary, the past and the future, what is and what might have been, what will be and what ought to be. Upon these very basic facts – which can be summarized in the traditional philosophical way, by

---

34   Rosalind Hursthouse, *On Virtue Ethics*, Oxford: OUP, 1998.

saying that we are rational animals – other and more remarkable facts depend. Unlike the animals, we have moral, aesthetic and religious experience; we pray to things visible and invisible; we laugh, sing and grieve; are indignant, approving and dismayed. And we relate to each other in a special way, through the give and take of practical reason, and its associated concepts of justice, duty and right. Human beings are actual or potential members of a moral community, in which each member enjoys sovereignty over his own affairs, so long as he accords an equal sovereignty to others. The concepts of right and duty regulate such a community, and ensure that disputes are settled in the first instance by negotiation and not by force. And with all this comes an immense burden of guilt. Morality and self-consciousness set us in judgement over ourselves, so that we see our actions and characters constantly from outside, judged by ourselves as we are by others. (It is part of the function of moral dialogue, and the concepts of duty, right and justice, to generate this external point of view.) We become cut off from our instincts, and even the spontaneous joy of fellowship is diminished by the screen of judgement through which it first must pass.

Animals rescue us from this predicament. Their lack of self-consciousness neutralizes our own possession of it, and their mute unembarrassability makes it possible to pour out on them the pent-up store of fellow feeling, without fear of judgement or reproach. At the same time, we are acutely aware of their moral incompetence. Their affection, if it can be won at all, is easily won, and based on nothing. However much a man may be loved by his dog, this love brings warmth and security, but no release from guilt. It is a love that implies no moral approval, and which leaves the character of its object unassessed and unendorsed. For many people in the conditions of civilized life, the relation with a pet is the best that can be achieved, by way of companionship. But it is a relation that is essentially one-sided, with one party speaking and acting for both. The master smiles into the eyes of his dog as into a mirror, and finds there no independent confirmation of his worth. For that very reason, a dog is a far easier companion than a person, and the temptation arises, first to believe that animals can be fully paid-up members of the human community, and second that all animals are really like our pets, with the same moral claims and the same need for consideration that characterize the animals on whom we depend for companionship. That which distinguishes us from the animals – our predicament as self-conscious and judging creatures – leads us constantly to discount the difference, to act as though it were a marginal consideration on which nothing hangs when it comes to the real ethical questions.

Richard Ryder even coined the word 'speciesism' to describe the sin of making moral distinctions between people and other animals, implying that this habit of discrimination is like racism and sexism. In other words, that it is a habit of moral discrimination, on the basis of morally irrelevant facts. Thanks to Peter Singer the word has caught on, and perhaps it is worth pausing to consider just how utterly misleading it is. It is not the difference of species that I endow with moral significance, when I distinguish people from other animals. It is rather the difference between a moral being, who lives as the subject and object of judgement, and a non-moral being, who merely lives. Maybe all moral beings belong to a single species: but it is not the species that I consider, when I distinguish the life and fulfilment of a person from the life and fulfilment of a dog. And if any distinctions are morally relevant, then surely the distinction between the moral and the non-moral being is one of them.

It is often objected that we do in fact make discriminations on grounds of species membership, since we afford to 'marginal humans', who lack the capacities that distinguish the moral being from the rest of nature, some, although not all, of the privileges of fully responsible people. For example we regard the killing of an idiot as a crime comparable to the killing of a normal person; we extend a duty of care and protection to the retarded, the brain-damaged and the vegetative that we withhold from animals more intelligent and more capable than they. To this I would respond that we do this because the human form is, for us, the outward sign and symbol of the moral life, and because we never wish to foreclose the possibility that each human body harbours, in whatever embryonic form, a personality. This reaction is part of piety; it may be hard to justify it in terms of the cold, hard, utilitarian reasoning that appeals to Peter Singer; but the fault lies in that cold, hard form of reasoning. Utilitarianism overlooks precisely what is so distinctive of our condition, which is our rooted disposition to understand ourselves as moral beings, bound in relations of accountability to others of our kind. We define human nature in terms of its normal development, along the trajectory of the personal and responsible life. That is the kind of thing that we are; and it is the kind to which even the tragically abnormal human being belongs, and from which dogs, cats, horses and all other animals with which we habitually have dealings are by their nature excluded.

This distinction comes immediately to life when we consider the question of eating. Whether or not we think that eating people is wrong, we certainly do not think that eating people is on a par with eating other animals. For most of us it is only some extreme emergency that would tempt us to partake of human flesh, and the habits of cannibals fill us with distaste. We can understand what they do if it is an expression of dire need; and we can also understand it as a kind of symbolism – a human sacrifice, for example, in which the gods are intimately concerned, or a way of triumphing over enemies. But we recoil from the idea that human beings might be on the daily menu along with cabbage, chicken, squirrel and lentils, with no noticeable stigma attached to choosing the first of those dishes.

The case brings to the fore two interesting issues: first that of the real distinction between humans and other animals, to which I have just referred as a metaphysical, rather than a merely natural distinction; second, that of the distinction between our attitude to the human body, even when dead, and our attitude to the bodies of other animals. Reason is apt to surrender in the face of our mortality, leaving us with peculiar residues of itself. These residues are emotions that cannot be easily understood in rational terms, and which we can rationalize, if at all, only through religious or quasi-religious conceptions – as when we speak of the sanctity of the human being, or the awe-inspiring nature of the human corpse. Such emotions belong to that philosophically neglected realm of the psyche which I have called piety. Although elephants and dolphins engage in behaviour which shows a partial resemblance to our feelings in the presence of the dead, the emotions with which we approach a corpse are emotions that only a self-conscious being can experience – so at least it seems to me – and which must be characterized in terms like 'awe', 'reverence' and 'anxiety'. The corpse is not to be carelessly touched, not to be defiled, not to be abused. It demands reverential treatment such as burial, and its former occupant surrounds it like an aura, demanding to be mourned. All this you will find beautifully described and evoked in the great scene between Achilles and Priam in the *Iliad*, when the old king comes to beg for Hector's desecrated body. Not that all cultures treat this predicament as the Homeric Greeks treated it. But in all cultures some form of piety is called forth by the human corpse. This is not some arbitrary or eliminable feature of our condition, but a non-rational consequence of being rational.

These non-rational feelings may also be, in another sense, quite reasonable. That is to say, it may be part of leading a good life that one acquires the habit of them. For example, it could be true – indeed, I think it is true – that we begin to heal the wounds of grief by cherishing the corpse of the person we have lost. And pious conduct, because it tends naturally to complete itself in ritual, brings the comfort of companionship in our time of need. In such ways we can imagine a perfectly good functional justification for these feelings which would, however, disappear if we thought of them in purely functional terms. Piety is justified by impious reasons, and exists only so long as we don't ask the reason why: indeed, that is its essence – a sense of duty, that does not question what it receives as commands.

So far as I know, people do not eat their pets, even when the pets belong to species that are commonly eaten. For pets are honorary members of the human community, and enjoy some imagined version of the nimbus that surrounds the human body – the nimbus that Michelangelo presented in his versions of the *pietà*. People bury their dogs and cats, often erecting tombstones over their bodies. And even when this seems absurd, some kind of piety is bestowed on an animal whose companionship has been enjoyed, when it is a companion no longer.

Pious feelings survive also in the religious prohibitions that in many cultures attach to the eating of meat. Anthropologists have wrestled fruitlessly with these strange codes, rigorously adhered to by Jews, Muslims and others, which permit the eating of meat and fish, while arbitrarily and vehemently banning this or that variety. The existence of these codes is a sure sign that more is at stake in our eating habits than the satisfaction of hunger. If God takes such an interest in what we eat, then this can only be because eating and ingesting are acts not of the body only, but of the soul. Interestingly, however, dietary codes do not tell us not to defile the corpses of other animals. They tell us not to defile *ourselves* by eating what is forbidden. They provide further confirmation of the dramatic way in which animals and people are distinguished in our feelings.

In discussing the rights and wrongs of meat-eating, we encounter the deep divide between us and other species twice over. First, there is the fact that we are moral beings. And then there is the related fact that eating, for us, is not what it is for the other animals. A person's encounter with food may be an occasion of festivity and celebration; it may also be deeply unsettling, compromising and humiliating. Eating has in every traditional society been regarded as a social, often a religious, act, embellished by ritual and enjoyed as a primary celebration of membership. Rational beings are nourished on conversation, taste, manners and hospitality, and to divorce food from these practices is to deprive it of its true significance.[35]

The special relation of people to their food finds emblematic expression in the face. Human beings have neither claws nor fangs. They do not eat by pressing their mouth to their food, but

---

35 On these issues see Leon Kass, *The Hungry Soul: Eating and the Perfection of Our Nature*, New York: The Free Press, 1994. Felipe Fernández-Armesto has added historical detail to Kass's argument in his *Food: A History*, London: Jonathan Cape, 2002.

by raising their food to their mouth, which is the organ of speech and therefore of reason. The mouth is the centre of the face, and it is in the face that the human person is most immediately encountered, in the form of looks and glances, smiles, grimaces and words. People therefore place their food into their mouths with special care, usually by means of an instrument that creates a distance between the food and the face, so that the glance, the smile and the self remain visible while eating.

Rational beings rejoice less in filling themselves than in the sight of food, table and guests dressed for a ceremonial offering. Their meals are also sacrifices, and anthropologists have occasionally argued that the origin of our carnivorous ways lies in the burnt offerings of ancient ritual. Only rational beings make gifts and it is the giving of food, usually as the central episode in a ceremony, that is the core of hospitality, and therefore of those actions through which we lay claim to our home and at the same time mutely apologize for owning it.

In the fast-food culture food is not given but taken, which is one reason why, in such a culture, nobody is properly 'at home'. The solitary stuffing of burgers, pizzas and 'TV dinners'; the disappearance of family meals and domestic cooking; the loss of table manners – all these tend to obscure the distinction between eating and feeding. And for many people vegetarianism is a roundabout way of restoring that distinction. Vegetables are gifts of the Earth: by eating them we re-establish contact with our roots. They offer a way of once again incorporating food into the moral life, hedging it in with moral scruples, and revitalizing the precious sense of shame.

I don't think there can be any vindication of meat-eating that does not engage with the deep feelings that prompt our dietary habits, and which also forbid them. Although I do not think that there is a compelling moral argument against meat-eating, I do believe that the onus lies on the carnivore to show that there is a way of incorporating meat into a life that respects the moral and spiritual realities, and which does not shame the human race, as it is shamed by the solitary 'caveman' gluttony of the burger-stuffer.

So how do we answer the question, whether eating animals is

wrong? How do we answer it, that is, from a point of view that recognizes the various sources of moral judgement, as I described them at the outset of this chapter? So far I have been discussing piety – the least amenable to reason of the motives on which the moral life is built. But the argument has also touched on one of the three pillars of moral judgement, as I see it: the concept of virtue. We can already see from what I have hinted at, that there might be a distinction between virtuous and vicious eating. Virtue is a matter of habit, but it is not an unconscious habit. It is the habit of behaving in creditable or honourable ways, in the face of temptation. Virtuous eating involves good manners – in other words behaviour that is considerate of others and which permits and facilitates the easy continuation of dialogue. Good manners prevent that sudden and disturbing eclipse of the person by the animal, as the fangs sink themselves into the mess on the plate.

But that is only the smallest part of it: the *sine qua non* that guarantees nothing. There is also the virtue of temperance: of eating the right amount at the right speed, and not giving way to gluttony. It is well known that carnivores have a tendency to intemperance, and that the results of this, in the steadily increasing size of the American variety, constitute a kind of offence against others which is all the greater in that the offender seems unable to notice the fact. Still, there is nothing about meat-eating that necessarily ties it to this kind of vicious behaviour, and the old and delicate art of *haute cuisine* is designed precisely to further the temperate enjoyment of meat, and its ceremonial place on the table.

But what of the dish itself? It is surely a part of virtue to consider what benefits and harms are promoted by your actions – not, I hasten to add, in the manner of the utilitarian, seeking a comprehensive balance sheet of pleasure and pain, but in the manner of the humane person, who wishes to promote kindness and to oppose cruelty – in other words to promote virtue over vice.

Advocates of virtue ethics often argue as though we could understand virtue without consulting the other pillar of moral judgement, which is the concept of obligation. I doubt that this severance of virtue from principle is really possible. The virtue of kindness, which we are now considering, cannot be understood without also invoking ideas of responsibility, duty and right. A person is not kind just by pouring out benefits indiscriminately on others, without regard for their respective claims. Or if you call this kindness, then kindness is not a virtue. As I understand it, kindness means treating with gentleness and consideration all those with whom you have dealings, while also fulfilling your obligations towards them. The person who treats his wife with careful consideration while at the same time being unfaithful to her is only apparently kind; and the person who gives all his money away while neglecting to retain enough of it to feed his children is not kind but profligate. Much work in what Kant called 'moral anthropology' is needed, if we are to make sense of the virtue of kindness, and in any plausible account we will surely conclude that it is not detachable from a right regard for responsibilities, and a conscientious desire to fulfil them.

The approach of virtue ethics does not, therefore, take us in a distinct direction, when it comes to the issue of meat-eating. On the contrary, it points back to the fundamental question of deontology: what are our obligations and do they permit us to eat animals?

If animals had rights then there would be absolute limits to the things that we could do to them. We could not, for example, kill them, breed them for our purposes, train them without their consent or take them into captivity. We certainly could not raise them for food, still less raise them in the kind of conditions that have become normal in the industrialized world. But the moral problem arises either because animals do not have rights, so that the principles that impede our invasions of other people do not serve to protect them, or because they have rights, but rights so differently ordered from those of humans, as to leave whole areas of human conduct towards them undetermined. I happen to think that the attribution of rights to animals is unhelpful, since it involves uprooting the concept of a right from the moral and legal practices that give it sense.[36] But, whether or not I am justified in that approach hardly matters. For the question concerns not *their*

---

36 See *Animal Rights and Wrongs*, op. cit.

rights but *our duties*. And if I am right even the proponent of virtue ethics must recognize the concept of duty or obligation as an indispensable part of ethical thinking, with a logic that is not straightforwardly derivable from the concept of the good life.

Obligations make distinctions. They bind me to some things, and leave me free from others. For example, I have an obligation to my daughter, to see that she is properly fed and educated, which I do not have to your daughter. Kindness is not shown by ignoring that obligation in order to satisfy the need of some stranger. On the contrary, that would be a sign of callousness, an inability to respond to real and legitimate claims.

Some obligations are undertaken: as when we promise something. Others arise independently of our choice, like the obligations to parents, to country and to neighbours. Others still arise by an invisible hand, to use Adam Smith's expression, from behaviour that has no such intention. Obligations to animals are often like this. The person who enjoys eating meat is putting himself into relation with the creatures on his plate. He is doing something which creates an obligation that he must fulfil. It would be a mark of callousness to ignore this obligation, to behave with complete indifference towards the life and sufferings of the creatures that he eats. But what exactly *is* the obligation?

Animals bred or kept for our uses are not honorary members of the moral community, as pets or 'companion animals' are. Nevertheless, the use that we make of them imposes a reciprocal duty to look after them, which spreads forward from the farmer to the slaughterer and from the slaughterer to the consumer, all of whom benefit from these animals, and all of whom must therefore assume some part of the duty of care. If these animals were moral beings then we could not, morally speaking, make use of them as we do – just as we cannot enslave human beings or breed them for food. And if the life of an animal bred for food were simply one long torment, the only relief from which is the final slaughter, we should certainly conclude the practice to be immoral. Utilitarians might disagree, since a utilitarian can justify any amount of suffering, provided the greater happiness is achieved by it. But that is one of the things that is wrong with utilitarianism. Moreover, until we have specified duties, moral judgement cannot begin, and duties cannot be assigned by the Greatest Happiness principle. Their ground lies in the past, not the future, and they cannot be overridden merely because some good can be achieved by disobeying them.

To criticize battery pig farming as violating a duty of care is surely right and proper. But the argument does nothing to condemn other livestock practices. There is surely scope, here, for some comparative judgements. Consider the traditional beef farmer, who fattens his calves for 30 months, keeping them on open pasture in the summer and in warm roomy barns in the winter, feeding them on grass, silage, beans and maize, attending to them in all their ailments, and sending them for slaughter, when the time comes, to the nearby slaughterhouse, where they are instantly despatched by a humane killer. Surely, such a farmer treats his cattle as well as cattle can be treated. Of course, he never asked them whether they wanted to live in his fields, or gave them the choice of lifestyle during their time there. But that is because he knows – from instinct rather than from any philosophical theory – that cattle cannot make such choices, and do not exist at the level of consciousness for which freedom and the lack of it are genuine realities.

Animals raised for meat are, for the most part, gregarious, gentle and dependent. They are unhappy in isolation and emotionally dependent on the proximity of their kind. In the winter they must be sheltered; in the summer, if they are lucky, they are out to grass, or (in the case of the pig and the chicken) free to roam in a place where they can hunt for scraps of food. Human standards of hygiene are alien to their nature and their affections, unlike ours, are general and transferable, without tragic overtones. Such animals, tended in the traditional way, by a farmer who houses them together in the winter and allows them to roam in the summer, are as happy as their nature allows. Assuming that their needs are satisfied, only two questions arise in the farmer's mind, which is when and how they should be killed – for that they must be killed is evident, this being the reason why they live. Death is not merely a moral question. There is an economic aspect which no farmer – and no consumer – can afford to ignore. And I suspect that those who believe that it is immoral to raise animals for meat have in mind the moment of death and the economic calculation that prompts us to cut short a life in its prime.

Here the metaphysical distinction between humans and other animals once again comes to the fore. Human beings are conscious of their lives as their own; they have ambitions, hopes and aspirations; they are fatally attached to others, who cannot be replaced in their affections but whose presence they feel as a need. Hence there is a real distinction, for a human being, between timely and untimely death. To be 'cut short' before one's time is a waste – even a tragedy. We lament the death of children and young people not merely because we lament the death of anyone, but because we believe that human beings are fulfilled by their achievements and not merely by their comforts.

No such thoughts apply to domestic cattle. To be killed at 30 months is not intrinsically more tragic than to be killed at 40, 50 or 60. And if the meat is at its best after 30 months, and if every month thereafter represents an economic loss, who will blame the farmer for choosing so early a death? In so doing he merely reflects the choice of the consumer, upon whose desires the whole trade in meat, and therefore the very existence of his animals, depends.

But what about the manner of death? That it should be quick is not in dispute. Nevertheless, there is a distinction between sudden death and death preceded by terror, and to the conscientious farmer, who has looked after his animals from day to day, living with them and providing for their needs, this terror is not merely unwelcome but a betrayal of trust and a dagger of accusation. Livestock farmers, therefore, prefer to see their animals despatched suddenly and humanely in the place where they have lived, by skilled slaughterers who know how to kill an animal without awakening it from its soporific routine.

Livestock farming is not merely an industry – it is a relation, in which man and animal are bound together to their mutual profit, and in which a human duty of care is nourished by an animal's mute recognition of dependency. There is something consoling and heart-warming in the proximity of contented herbivores, in the rituals of feeding them, catching them, and coaxing them from field to field. This partly explains why people will continue in this time-consuming, exhausting and ill-paid occupation, resisting the attempts by bureaucrats and agribusinesses to drive them to extinction. Anybody who cares for animals ought to see this kind of husbandry as a complex moral good, to be defended on the one hand against those who would forbid the eating of meat altogether, and on the other hand against those carnivores who prefer the unseen suffering of the battery farm and the factory abattoir to the merest suggestion of a personal risk.

The life of the cattle farmer is not an easy life, nor is the relation between man and animal always as harmonious as it appears in the numerous children's books devoted to life on the farm. Nevertheless, as with all forms of husbandry, cattle farming should be seen in its full context – and that means, as a feature of the total ecology of the countryside. Traditional livestock farming involves the maintenance of pastureland, properly enclosed with walls or hedges. Wildlife habitats spring up as the near-automatic by-products of the boundaries and shady places required by cattle. This kind of farming has shaped the English landscape, ensuring that it retains its dual character as producer of human food and complex wildlife habitat, with a beauty that is inextricably connected to its multifarious life. In this way, what is, from the point of view of agribusiness, an extremely wasteful use of land, becomes, from the point of view of the rest of us – both human and animal – one of the kindest uses of land yet devised.

I have abbreviated the story. But it could be expanded into a full vindication of livestock farming, as conferring benefits on all those, the animals included, who are part of it. When animals raised for their meat are properly looked after, when all duties of care are fulfilled, and when the demands of sympathy and piety are respected, the practice cannot be criticized except from a premise – the premise of animal rights – which I believe to be incoherent. Of course, the result of raising animals in this way will change the character of meat-eating, which will become not only more expensive, but more ceremonial – as it was before the battery farm. The animal brought to the table will have enjoyed the friendship and protection of the one who nurtured him, and his death will be like the ritual sacrifices described in the Bible and Homeric literature – a *singling out* of a victim, for an important office to which a kind of honour is attached.

Such it seems to me would be the life of the virtuous carnivore, the one who is prepared to eat only his friends. The real force of the vegetarian argument stems, I believe, from a revulsion at the vicious carnivore: the meat-eating character as this has evolved in these days of gluttony and indulgence. And it is entirely true that the indifference of modern carnivores to the methods used to reduce the cost of their habit is a morally repulsive characteristic against which it is wholly natural to rebel. The repulsiveness is enhanced by the solipsistic fast-food culture, and by the removal of food from its central place in domestic life and in the winning of friends. From Homer to Zola meat has been described as the focus of hospitality, the primordial gift to the stranger, the eruption into the world of human conflict of the divine spirit of peace. Take all that away, reduce meat to an object of solitary greed like chocolate, and the question naturally arises: why should *life* be sacrificed, just for this?

As I indicated, this question has a religious dimension. From the point of view of morality it has a clear and rational answer: namely, that the life that is sacrificed would not exist, but for the sacrifice. A great number of animals owe their lives to our intention to eat them. And their lives are (or can easily be made to be) comfortable and satisfying in the way that few lives led in the wild could possibly be. If we value animal life and animal comfort, therefore, we should endorse our carnivorous habits, provided it really is *life*, and not living death, on which those habits feed. From the point of view of religion, however, the question presents a challenge. It is asking the burger-stuffer to *come clean*; to show just why it is that his greed should be indulged in this way, and just where he fits into the scheme of things, that he can presume to kill again and again for the sake of a solitary pleasure that creates and sustains no moral ties. To such a question it is always possible to respond with a shrug of the shoulders. But it is a real question, one of many that people now ask, as the old forms of piety dwindle. Piety is the remedy for religious guilt, and to this emotion we are all witting or unwitting heirs. And I suspect that people become vegetarians for precisely that reason: that by doing so they overcome the residue of guilt that attaches to every form of hubris, and in particular to the hubris of human freedom.

I believe, however, that there is another remedy, and one more in keeping with the Judaeo-Christian tradition. We should not abandon our meat-eating habits, but *remoralize* them, by incorporating them into affectionate human relations, and using them in the true Homeric manner, as instruments of hospitality, conviviality and peace. That was the remedy practised by our parents, with their traditional 'Sunday roast' coming always at midday, after they had given thanks. The lifestyle associated with the Sunday roast involves sacrifices that those brought up on fast food are unused to making – mealtimes, manners, dinner-table conversation and the art of cookery itself. But all those things form part of a complex human good, and I cannot help thinking that, when added to the ecological benefits of small-scale livestock farming, they secure for us an honourable place in the scheme of things, and neutralize more effectively than the vegetarian alternative, our inherited burden of guilt.

Furthermore, I would suggest not only that it is permissible for those who care about animals to eat meat; they have a duty to do so. If meat-eating should ever become confined to those who do not care about animal suffering then compassionate farming would cease. All animals would be kept in battery conditions and the righteous vegetarians would exert no economic pressure on farmers to change their ways. Where there are conscientious carnivores, however, there is a motive to raise animals kindly. And conscientious carnivores can show their depraved contemporaries that it is possible to ease one's conscience by spending more on one's meat. Bit by bit the news would get around, that there is a right and a wrong way to eat; and – failing some *coup d'état* by censorious vegetarians – the process would be set in motion, that would bring battery farming to an end. Duty requires us, therefore, to eat our friends.

4

Dying Quietly

Suppose John, who is terminally ill and suffering, has kept a lethal dose of some drug in order to put an end to his life in circumstances like these. But suppose that, being too weak to move, John were to beg his friend Alfred to administer the drug. Alfred does so out of compassion, but reluctantly and with no expectation of gain. Here we would surely not accuse Alfred of killing John. It is John himself who made the relevant decision, and called on Alfred, out of friendship and compassion, to help him to do what he could no longer do alone. The case is one of assisted suicide, in extenuating circumstances that remove the suggestion of criminal intent.

Contrast the case of John's wife Helen, who expects to inherit, who has no knowledge that John has decided to die if he can, but who knows of the lethal drug and surreptitiously slips it into her husband's tea, hoping to get off on a plea of mercy killing. Here Helen is the initiator of the process that leads to John's death. She, and not he, took the relevant decision, and her motives were little different from those of any normal self-interested murderer. Even if John is terminally ill and hoping for just this kind of assistance, this makes no difference to the nature of Helen's act.

As such examples show, the criminal law forbids or permits actions, not results. An action is not simply a bodily movement. It is a process originating in a state of mind. Hence every serious crime involves both *actus reus* and *mens rea* – the act performed and the state of mind that makes it criminal. This state of mind may not involve any explicit intention: there can be criminal negligence, criminal indifference and criminal motives that fall short of a settled decision. Moreover, the description of intentions is not always easy, as the two imaginary cases illustrate. Both Alfred and Helen intend John's death. But while Helen *kills* John, Alfred merely assists John's suicide. While Helen intends John's death in her own interests, Alfred intends it only in the interests of John. In most matters relevant to moral and legal judgement, Alfred's intention and Helen's are quite distinct. To give the full account of the intention in cases like this is also to lay down the grounds for a judgement of responsibility. Helen is responsible for John's death; Alfred not, or at least not entirely. More: Helen is to blame for John's death. In the case of Alfred, blame is more diffi-cult to assign. Moreover, blame can be incurred even for an effect that is unintended. If you neglect your child and he dies you could be to blame for his death, even if you did not intend it.

The examples also show how legal and moral blame diverge. You can be legally blamed for an action that is morally blameless; many people think that mercy killing comes into this category. And you can be morally blamed for what is legally blameless, as in the case of adultery or abortion. Settling the question of legal blame in a case like Alfred's might be far easier than settling the question of whether he is also to blame from the point of view of moral judgement.

On the other hand, we should not suppose that legal and moral judgement are entirely independent. The criminal law depends upon moral intuitions and a moral consensus. When the intu-itions are weak and the consensus fragile, the law loses its force. This is what happened in the 1960s, in the matter of the laws governing sexual conduct, which had to be relaxed when there was no longer a consensus in favour of enforcing them. Conversely a strong moral consensus will demand legal enforce-ment: this is happening now in the sphere of animal welfare.

There are also controversial areas, where moral intuitions are both strong and conflicting, as they are in the matter of abortion. The general view of liberal democracies is that the law should not, in such a case, take sides. The law does not exist to enforce controversial moral views against those who disagree with them, but to reconcile differences and establish government by consent. It is not always easy to achieve those goals. But it is certain that we will not achieve them, if we regard the law as open to capture by 'special moral interests', so as to become a weapon wielded by one section of the community against another. This has happened in this country from time to time: most recently in the ban on hunting. But this kind of puritanical legislation goes against one of the background assumptions of liberal democratic government.

Nevertheless, where there is a real and pressing moral consensus, the law will normally enforce it. People do not regard a law as tyrannical if it forbids what they regard as impermissible. And when the law fails to enforce shared moral values it loses credibility. This too has happened recently, in the matter of self-defence and burglary. The moral consensus is that it is permissible to respond to a threat with force, if the intention is to defend your life, limb or property. People recognize that such force can be excessive and that violent homeowners should not be provided with the excuse to let fly at harmless intruders. Nevertheless, they are on the side of the one who is invaded, and are not eager to deprive him of the weapons that he might need to defend himself. If the law punishes him for using those weapons, then the law is felt to be imposing the morality of liberal judges on those who live, as they must live, by another and more durable standard. Laws which, in that way, overrule the majority consensus in the interests of a minority point of view, are regarded as divisive and oppressive. And when laws are so viewed the function of law, as an instrument of social reconciliation, is seriously jeopardized. The view of law as a system of edicts, designed to impose the will of a ruling class, clique or party, is entirely alien to our English tradition. For us, inheritors of the common law, law is the ultimate arbitrator in our disputes, answerable only to impartial justice. Edicts designed to control us or to amend our ways, rather than to settle our conflicts, bring the law into disrepute. For they treat the law as another form of coercion, different from that of the mafia or the gang only in having the authority of parliament.

It is clear from those brief considerations that the question of the relation between morality and law is as urgent as it is deep and difficult. To argue with John Stuart Mill that the function of the law is to guarantee the greatest liberty of the individual, including the liberty to dissent from majority moral practice, is to detach the law from its bedrock in moral consensus. To argue with Mill's opponent, Sir James Fitzjames Stephen, that the function of law is to uphold the moral order and to provide leadership in the face of moral decay, is to jeopardize the impartiality of the law, and to provide no protection to the dissenter. We need to steer a middle course here. People need freedom; but without the underlying consensus, freedom is at risk. People also need a shared moral order; but without the freedom to dissent from it, their participation may be no better than a sham. When it comes to controversial areas, where society is genuinely divided in its moral views, the law should retreat from direct involvement, and attempt to find ways in which differences can be reconciled and compromises achieved. That has been the ruling principle in matters of sexual conduct: and the question that troubles many people today is whether this principle can be extended to cover euthanasia, assisted suicide, mercy killing and the other ways in which, in our new conditions, we find ourselves tempted to take the side of death.

I shall begin from a very one-sided perspective. According to this perspective there may come a point in any person's life in which it would be better not to go on: pain and incapacity are no longer to be endured, and there is nothing to look forward to save more of the same and worse. In these circumstances, it might be argued, death is the best thing that could happen to the sufferer, and anybody who assists him in achieving it is doing him a favour while harming no one else. A law that nevertheless forbids such assistance does no good and much potential harm. It ought therefore to be abolished.

The argument depends upon two assumptions. First, that a law is justified by considering costs and benefits. Second, that the only relevant costs and benefits in the case of euthanasia are the suffering of the victim, the benefit to him of being released from it, the absence of any cost borne by others near to him and the potential benefit to these others of being released from an onerous and perhaps intolerable burden of care.

Both those assumptions are questionable. Some will argue that cost-benefit analysis is not the only way to justify or criticize law, and indeed that it may be wholly misconceived to think in such terms, when the law touches on some fundamental moral prohibition. Consider the laws that forbid us to desecrate graves or to dig up and make illicit use of corpses. Someone who criticized these laws, on the grounds that the dead cannot be harmed, and that no one else is harmed when someone nevertheless finds a use for them, has failed to see what is at stake. These laws exist to protect and enforce a moral consensus, one that we might find hard to justify except in religious terms, but which stems from an attitude deeply implanted in the human soul – the attitude that I have called piety. And it could be that our laws forbidding euthanasia are similar, in engaging with a deeply felt prohibition that has nothing directly to do with the costs and benefits of obeying it.

The second assumption can also be questioned. Even if we consider cost-benefit analysis to be the ultimate recourse of jurisprudence, we should be aware that all actions – and especially those that touch on our deeper and more mysterious instincts – have hidden costs, and that often these costs are incalculable. Abolishing the law against euthanasia may bring benefits to those who suffer from painful and incurable illnesses, and to those obliged to look after them. But it will also change our collective perception of death. It will lessen the awe with which the deliberate killing of a human being is viewed; it will instil a habit of calculation where previously only absolutes guided our conduct; and in general it will make death and dying both easier to deal with and easier to bring about. Whether these changes of attitude will benefit human societies or damage them is a matter over which we may reasonably disagree. But the likelihood – indeed the inevitability – of their occurrence is sufficient to refute the assumption that no costs or benefits attach to euthanasia besides those immediately experienced by the sufferer and those near to him.

Those who wish to reform the law, so as to extend a measure of permission towards those who assist the deaths of the incurably ill, ought therefore to be wary of advancing a cost-benefit account of legislation. Even if it is true that the ultimate justification of a law lies in the balance of benefits achieved over costs incurred, the calculation of these factors lies usually so much beyond our capacity, that only in retrospect will we be able to make a guess at them. As in the case of moral judgement, we are guided in our search for law by conceptions that cannot easily be reduced to some utilitarian calculus. The best advice to the law reformer, therefore, is to go carefully, to make only incontestable assumptions, and to endeavour to set out the human problem in its full complexity before attempting a legislative answer to it. This advice is not often followed, for the simple reason that people are always impatient for reform whenever they find their ambitions impeded by the law, and are always reluctant to accept – what may be glaringly obvious to others – that the law exists precisely to impede their ambitions. Thus, when people pressed for a reform of the law regarding abortion, so as to make abortion legal during the first three months of pregnancy, no attempt was made to achieve a consensual understanding of our duties towards children in the womb; no attempt was made to assess the impact of legalizing abortion during the first three months on our attitude to abortions conducted at some later stage of pregnancy; no attempt was made to assess the long-term changes in people's attitude to children induced by the practice of so easily disposing of them before they have a chance to look us in the eyes. All the deep, difficult and important questions were set aside, in the interests of those whose ambitions were obstructed by the existing law. Yet the law existed precisely to obstruct those ambitions, just as the law against burglary exists to obstruct the ambitions of the burglar. As a result, the reform of the law has generated an entirely new sense of disquiet, as the public conscience awakens to the reality of mass abortion.

Although there are good arguments on both sides of the abortion debate, it is now clear that the law was reformed too hastily and in response to pressure from only one set of interests and attitudes. Pressure for reform of the law regarding euthanasia likewise reflects a particular set of interests and attitudes, and it is wise to examine those interests and attitudes, to ascertain how widely they are distributed in modern societies, and the extent to which they are really beneficial to society as a whole. Here is where a little philosophical reflection is called for.

The conflict over abortion focuses on the nature and meaning of life; that over euthanasia on the nature and meaning of death. There are, roughly speaking, three approaches to death – the religious, the scientific and the philosophical – and they are not obviously compatible. The religious approach sees death as a point of transition, the entry into another world and the occasion of judgement. The scientific approach sees death as the extinction of the organism, the point at which the human being ceases and no longer has a care in the world or a care out of it. The philosophical approach sees death as a boundary to our projects, an envelope in which life is enfolded and which casts all our pleasures in its own peculiar light. Death, for the philosopher, is something to be understood, in the way that we understand a person, a text or a work of art – by discerning what it means.

Both the civilian and the common-law traditions have developed during centuries of religious consensus and under the influence of Christian ideas of the nature and goal of human life. Hence the religious view of death has been assumed, though never explicitly stated, by our laws. On this view death is the human being's entry into judgement and into the world to come; to kill another is not merely to violate God's law. It is also to send him prematurely to judgement, and thereby to affect his chances of eternal happiness. Whatever sufferings precede death they are of little or no significance compared with the life thereafter, and to shorten another's life merely in order to alleviate suffering is to meddle with the eternal for the sake of the temporal and the divinely ordained for the sake of the humanly desired.

Those abstract and theological ideas are connected with a more concrete and human experience, which is that of the sacred nature of human life. The human being, conceived in the religious way, is the vehicle of a human soul and as such is both sacred in himself and a symbol of God's holy purpose. The human form is therefore susceptible to desecration and to sacrilegious use. Certain moments in human life – birth, death and reproduction – present the sanctity of human life as an immediate and vivid perception. We look on them with awe and reverence or, if we don't, this is a fault and an offence against God. The correct response to these things, for the religious spirit, is to acknowledge and protect their sacred character – by setting them within a ceremonial and religious context, and by recognizing that they are expressions of a divine and inscrutable purpose and not merely of our own fleeting interests.

This aspect of the religious view has its counterpart in the minds of unbelievers. Even atheists and agnostics feel the need to approach the dead with awe and reverence, and to mark their passing with some ceremonial acknowledgement of the inscrutable mystery that has removed them for ever from the world that they shared. The sense of the sacred lies deeper than the beliefs that clarify its meaning, and will therefore survive them. Even when the religious worldview wanes, as it is waning in Western societies today, people will not necessarily be ready to accept laws that fly in the face of sacred prohibitions or which show a fundamentally sacrilegious approach to the human person. That is why, sexual liberation notwithstanding, we still hope that the law will put some kind of brake upon pornography, obscenity and the sexualization of children. And it is why agnostics and atheists can sympathize with the reluctance that believers feel to condone either abortion or euthanasia, and why they too may hope for legislation that conserves what can be saved, in a secular age, of the instinctive reverence for life.

In sharp distinction to the religious view of death is the view promoted by science. According to this view death is something that occurs to every living organism when its systems collapse. The death of a human being is a biological event no different in principle from the death of a dog, a lobster or an oak tree. It may be an occasion of grief to others, but to the sufferer himself it is merely the end of things, the final full stop to his pains. Life after death is neither observed nor observable, and science can take no account of it.

The scientific and religious views can be reconciled, albeit with difficulty, in a single consciousness. You could believe that the fate of the human soul, viewed from the religious perspective, has little or nothing to do with the fate of the human body, viewed from the perspective of science. Nevertheless, the scientific vision is commonly understood as eroding and displacing the religious perspective, and when people accept it, they find it difficult to believe in life after death. Hence they begin to accept the loss incurred through death as absolute and permanent. In reaction they protect themselves against grief. Permanent loss is hard to bear, if it is the loss of something precious. By devaluing human life, you make it easier to accept the loss of it. Paradoxically, therefore, the scientific perspective which seems to give back death's sting has led to a certain dwindling in our lamentations, and a willingness to treat death more lightly. Moreover science, which clarifies facts, mystifies values. It is difficult for someone who adopts the frame of mind recommended by Richard Dawkins to find any other basis for morality than the cost-benefit analysis of the utilitarians. A calculating approach to death replaces the sacred awe that had for so long filled our thoughts with prohibitions. It begins to seem irrational – even immoral – to deprive the terminally ill of the only known refuge from their sufferings. What is the point of those extra weeks of life, when all the good of life is over? This is an attitude eloquently – and humanely – expressed by the Dutch doctor Johan Kietzer in *Dancing with Dr D*, a book relating his experiences in a Dutch hospice for the terminally ill, where euthanasia is regularly practised.

Finally, there is the philosophical perspective on death – the perspective that tries to find a meaning in this fate to which we all are doomed. Now there is no consensus among philosophers as to how we should approach death or what significance it has for us when living. But there is a shared assumption among all who have addressed the matter, that the truth about death is not exhaustively contained in the scientific view of it, and that death, if it is to be properly viewed by rational beings such as we are, must be *understood*, in the way that life is understood by the one who seeks to live righteously. The task of philosophy is to discover a meaning in death, and to derive from that meaning some guidance as to how we might live with our mortality and cease to despair at the thought of it.

The first thing that a philosopher is likely to remark upon is the great difference that exists, between a society in which death is accepted and the dead duly catered for, and one in which death is taboo and the dead put out of mind. In the first kind of society, the dead are still present among the living – their graves are tended, their counsels are sought and their memory is hallowed. Libations are poured to them, and to all the ceremonies in which life is applauded and enjoyed, they too are invited. Such societies do not regard death with quite the horror that we regard it, and the presence of the dead seems to add dignity and decorum to the social events staged by the living. A society that denies death – and ours seems to be moving in that direction – loses itself in sensual pleasures, ceases to cultivate the virtues, regards death as unmentionable and the attempt to confront it as absurd.

The philosopher will be awakened by this observation to the role of death in giving sense and continuity to human social institutions. People who acknowledge the presence of the dead and the duty to respect them see their own lives in another way. They are trustees of the benefits which they owe to the dead. Their attitude to the dead is mirrored in their attitude to the unborn: absent generations, for them, deserve respect, and the fact of being alive carries with it an obligation to pass on to the next generation what was received from the last. In short, respect for the dead is a foundation of social responsibility and a motive to care for the future.

The second thing a philosopher is likely to remark on is that the scientific view of death does not render us powerless in the face of it. After all, we have a scientific view of life, yet life still has a meaning for us. We can view human beings as science views them, as a bundle of cells governed by a network of neurones, and still recognize that human beings are distinct from the rest of nature in being objects of judgement, with moral and personal attributes that cannot be summarized in merely biological terms. In just that way we can see death as the cessation of an organic process, and at the same time as an event in the life of a moral being – one towards which both he and we might take up a personal stance. In a tragedy the death of the hero is a biological event; but it is also a moral event, with a complex meaning that must be understood through moral ideas. And tragedies show us that we can find, in another's death, both the end and the meaning of his life – as we find meaning in the death of Romeo and Juliet. The two lovers in Shakespeare's play give proof of their love through their death, and as a result become beautiful in our eyes. Their death shines a light back across their life and ennobles the love that led to it. Maybe we could all live in such a way, and maybe if we did so we should view death not as a cessation but as a boundary, a limit, which gives meaning to the events that lead up to it.

The third thing that a philosopher is likely to notice is that there is a distinction between the first-person and the third-person view of death. My death is not simply, for me, the death of RS, the event about which you might read in an obituary. It is a vast crisis, standing athwart my life and commanding me to prepare for it. I am prompted to philosophical reflection of another kind by this first-person perspective. Every death prompts the search for meaning – especially the death of someone loved. But my death challenges me in another way: its inevitability is like a command – namely, live your life so that this will be a part of it and not just an end to it. St Paul reminds us that 'in the midst of life we are in death', meaning that our normal ways of living forbid us to plan either the time or the manner of our extinction. Yet we need to live in such a way that death, when it comes, is not a catastrophe but (if possible) a culmination – a conclusion to our actions that can be read back into all that preceded it and show it to be worthwhile. Such was the hero's death as envisaged in the ancient world, and while the hero had to put death out of mind until the very last moment, he was also aware that there was a right way to die and that life would be meaningful and even happy if it was rightly concluded.

The human need to find a meaning in death should be borne in mind when we consider the question of suicide. There is all the difference in the world between the person who commits suicide in order to avoid a certain and far more painful death – like those unfortunates who threw themselves from the Twin Towers on 11 September 2001 – and the person who commits suicide as a moral gesture, like the noble suicides of Japan.[37] And there is as great a difference again between that last case, in which the suicide attempts to clear his moral record by a self-transcending gesture, and the 'life of suicide' described by Leslie Farber, in which a person flaunts his own death as a standing rebuke to a world that has failed to value him.[38] And assisting suicide is a very different action in those three cases, and almost certainly a crime in the third of them.

The philosophical quest for a meaning in death may be unsuccessful, or successful only locally. But it is a quest on which all thinking people spontaneously embark, and which therefore inevitably influences their way of seeing things. This quest for meaning is bound to influence our view of euthanasia, assisted suicide and the like, and if the quest is in conflict with the scientific and utilitarian approach then we can be sure that we will not be satisfied by legal reforms that are based on nothing more substantial than science. Hence the waning of the religious worldview will not of itself open the way to euthanasia, nor will a new 'scientific' consensus emerge to replace the old moral consensus that derived from the Christian religion and which is embedded in our common law. The old prohibitions will survive, not as religious commandments, but as exhortations to be serious, to treat death as it must be treated, if life is to command our respect. If people hesitate to amend the laws regarding assisted suicide and euthanasia, therefore, it is not only because religious prohibitions still exert their sway. It is because some vestige of the philosophical approach to death governs their thinking, and because, like the philosopher, they are not satisfied that science is the answer.

But what guidance can philosophy offer to legal reformers, other than the advice already given, to go slowly and circum-

37 See Ivan Morris, *The Nobility of Failure: Tragic Heroes in the History of Japan*, New York: Holt, Rinehart and Winston, 1975.
38 See Leslie Farber, 'Despair and the Life of Suicide', in *The Ways of the Will*, New York: Basic Books, 2000.

spectly about their business? First, it is wise to remember that attitudes to death and dying are changing, not only because of the waning of religious faith and the impact of science, but also because of changes in the cycle of human life. Modern medicine and modern nutrition have vastly increased life-expectancy, and the evidence is that, failing some catastrophe, people will live longer from year to year.

Second, given that fact, it is more than ever necessary for us to incorporate death into our life plans. We need to recognize the value of timely death and the futility of living beyond the point where anyone will mourn our passing. Whatever our view of the afterlife and the promises and threats of religion, we must recognize that happiness on Earth is available only through giving and receiving affection. From the first-person perspective the critical question is not that of terminal illness and the suffering that it involves. After all, suffering can usually be alleviated, and a person can be terminally ill even though fully capable of giving and receiving love. The critical question is longevity itself, which has brought about a situation in which we all have something to fear worse than death, namely the living death of the loveless.

Third, the sense of the sanctity of human life can be damaged just as much by longevity as by a permissive approach to abortion and euthanasia. Our respect for human life is continuous with our desire and capacity to relate to it. A world in which increasingly many human beings are without affectionate relations with their kind, persisting as burdens to be carried rather than companions to be enjoyed, will be a world in which human life seems far less precious than it seems to us today. The traditional respect for age and the view of age as a repository of wisdom and authority will both dwindle. Old people will be regarded increasingly as a nuisance. Moreover, because their numbers will be growing and their legal rights will be in no way diminished by their decrepitude, they will soon be majority shareholders in all public and most private goods. They will be sitting on the collective assets of mankind, preventing the young from owning them, and maybe waving their wills in the face of their heirs, in the hope of attracting attention. The situation could rapidly degenerate, to the point

where the younger members of society turn on the geriatrics and
compel them to get off the planet. And when that happens the
effect will resemble that already witnessed in the case of abortion:
the age at which geriatrics can be legally despatched across the
Styx will be constantly lowered, just as the age of permissible
abortion has been constantly raised. Eventually we will be back
where we started, with life expectancy reduced to three score
years and ten, though with euthanasia as the usual form of extinction.

Maybe that is slightly exaggerated. Still, it sits comfortably
with what we know of human nature, and therefore uncomfort-
ably with the normal conscience. Whatever reforms we contemplate, we must preserve the core prohibitions, the inherited fund
of reverence and the sense of the distinctiveness, the 'apartness'
and the non-negotiable worth of the individual human life. Lose
those things, and we lose everything upon which the law might
build in creating a passage through this dangerous territory. We
must also recognize, however, that an over-zealous attachment to
life is also a threat to its value. Death is not something to be
avoided at all costs, but a cost to be offset by benefits – including
the benefit of living and dying in a condition of mutual affection.
And here is where a little philosophy can help. For love – at least
the love that we know in this earthly realm – is a relation between
dying things and owes all its poignancy and consoling power to
the frailty and fleetingness against which it is the only remedy. We
should not allow the law to shield us from our mortality, or from
the fragility without which we could hardly be loved. Any emen-
dation to the laws governing medical treatment should be
designed not to shield us from death, but to protect the value of
human life against 'medical erosion', as one might call it. If people
are kept alive by medicines beyond the point when love expires,
and then killed by medicines in a deliberate plan to get rid of
them, we shall experience a steady erosion of the sense of human
life as a thing apart, and of death as its illuminated boundary.

It seems to me, therefore, that any reform to the law must be
one that shields us from the adverse effects of medicine itself –
one that enables us to restore the humane and commonsensical

relation between doctor and patient, that prevailed in the days before medicine took over. While no one then spoke of a right to euthanasia or assisted suicide, there was nevertheless a shared and tacit understanding that a patient could refuse treatment, that a doctor was entitled to relieve the sufferings of those who were terminally ill, and that, if relieving suffering entailed shortening life, this was not necessarily a cost to be avoided. The doctor who placed the extra dose of morphine at his patient's bedside, wishing thereby to ease the sufferer's passage from this world, received the grateful thanks of all involved, who regarded this small transaction as no real business of the law.

Unfortunately, those days of shared understandings and tacit agreements are over. Medical advances have changed our conception of the doctor's role, and the current clamour for 'patients' rights' means that people look to the law for guidance, in an area where it might be best if the law kept quiet. Personally, I have always trusted the spirit of the old common law, and the law of equity, to find real solutions to the questions posed by unforeseen and rapid social change. And I have always doubted the competence of parliament to solve such questions by statute. But for a variety of reasons only a vestige of the common law remains to us, and judges have little or no freedom of manoeuvre, when confronting cases like those that I considered at the beginning of this chapter. We are unavoidably faced, therefore, with the prospect of legal reform by parliament. What might have passed unnoticed into custom, must now be made explicit as a statutory right.

But should there be a right to euthanasia or a right to assisted suicide? It seems to me dangerous to create such rights, and this for two reasons. The first is a general worry, shared by many people today, about 'rights inflation'. We all have an interest in health, but to say that I have a *right* to health is to elevate *my health* into *your duty*. In general to fill the world with rights is to fill it with duties, and that means to create a growing, intolerable and possibly contradictory burden that neither the citizens as a whole, nor the government which is their favourite scapegoat, can discharge. A right to euthanasia will put doctors in an impossible quandary, should they believe, as surely many of them believe, that they have no duty to assist suicide in any form. It will be the subject of complex and distasteful litigation. And it will serve further to discredit the notion of a 'right', in the eyes of ordinary people. Second, this right will almost certainly be abused by those who stand to benefit from a death. It will be difficult to prove, after the death, that the deceased had not been exercising his legal right to die; at the same time, however, a question mark will be raised over every inheritance which has euthanasia as its cause. Again massive litigation will follow.

Furthermore, the invention of a right to euthanasia is unnecessary to achieve what must surely be the reasonable goal, of relieving suffering and protecting human dignity. All that is necessary is a return to what was once normal practice. We should respect those who refuse treatment, and who choose palliatives in the place of cures. Someone with the good fortune to contract an illness that will lead quickly and relatively painlessly to a death that is neither premature nor tardy, should be permitted to say farewell to his nearest and dearest, and to prepare his departure. It might be useful to lay down legal principles, which compel doctors to explain to their seriously ill patients, that they still have a choice, and that by refusing treatment and choosing palliatives they will both hasten their death and relieve their suffering. Such a law would create the conditions in which the tyranny of medicine might be broken – conditions in which people will once again recognize that death is not a calamity to be postponed for as long as possible, but a natural event for which one must prepare. The habit of timely death might then become engrained, and love restored between the elderly who possess the world, and their progeny anxious for a share in it.

As for euthanasia, this would present exactly the problems, in the world that I envisage, that it presents today. And maybe that is as it should be. Not every moral problem is soluble, and sometimes the insoluble nature of the problem reflects what is deepest and most valuable in the life that gives rise to it. Going back to the examples from which I began, it seems to me that the right approach of the law, in a case like Alfred's, is to withdraw, not by expressly permitting assisted suicide, but by allowing certain defences to a charge of manslaughter. By keeping in place the root idea – that it is a crime intentionally to bring about another person's death – while allowing certain defences adapted to the problematic cases, we enable the law to preserve its impartial attitude, and to leave the individual conscience in charge.

5

Meaningful Marriage

An institution can be looked at from outside, with the eyes of an anthropologist, who observes its social function. Or it can be looked at from inside, with the eyes of a participant, whose life it transforms. And what is observable from one perspective may not be observable from the other. The anthropologist who studies the seasonal war-making of a tribe may understand this institution as a way of securing territory, a way of controlling population and a way of reaching a renewable equilibrium with neighbours. The warrior understands the institution in quite another way. For him it is a source of brotherhood, a mystical affirmation of identity between himself and the tribe and a call to his soul from 'ancestral voices'. The concepts used by the anthropologist – social function, solidarity, ideology and so on – make no contact with the warrior's experience. If he were to make use of these concepts in describing what he feels, he would immediately cease to feel it. And the concepts that inform the warrior's self-understanding – brotherhood, destiny, sacred obligation – play no part in the anthropologist's explanation of what the warrior does.

This does not mean that the two people are entirely opaque to each other. Maybe, by an act of *Verstehen*, the anthropologist can enter into the experience of the man he studies, and imagine what it is like to see the world as he sees it. Maybe the tribesman can stand back sufficiently from his situation to envisage how it might be understood and explained by someone who was outside the fold of membership. Nevertheless, the two assign different and incommensurable values to the institution of seasonal warfare, and criticism offered from one perspective might have no bearing on the values that inform the other. For the anthropologist the institution is justified by its function, and if it becomes dysfunctional, then it loses its rationale. For the warrior the institution is justified by the sacred obligations on which it rests, and only if those obligations are rescinded can it be allowed to decay.

This mismatch between external and internal perspectives has been frequently remarked upon, and not only in the context of anthropology. We encounter it in moral philosophy, in the conflict between consequentialism, which sees ethics as policy directed towards an external goal, and the deontological perspective that sees ethics in terms of absolute rights and duties. We encounter it in literature, in the contrast between the author's perspective and the values and motives of his characters. We encounter a version of it, too, in ourselves. For, as sophisticated modern people, we are in the habit of looking on our own values as though they were not ours at all, but the values of some curious stranger, who needs to be put in context and viewed from some fastidious height. We are all familiar with that Prufrock feeling, which reminds us in the midst of our warmest passions that we are perhaps wrong to presume, wrong to assume.

Indeed, it is arguable that the contrast between the two perspectives lies in the nature of things. A person is both I and he, both free subject and determined object, both rational chooser and predictable animal. We can see ourselves in either way, a possibility from which Kant derived his startling vision of our moral and metaphysical predicament. But it is perhaps a distinguishing mark of the modern condition that we are so easily tempted away from the first-person viewpoint to that other and more alienated posture, that turns self into other and choice into fate.

This has a bearing, I believe, on the current debates over marriage. For marriage is one of those institutions that we spontaneously see both from outside, in terms of its social function, and from inside, in terms of the moral and spiritual condition that it creates. No honest anthropologist can fail to acknowledge the functional importance of marriage. In all observed societies some form of marriage exists, as the means whereby the work of one generation is dedicated to the well-being of the next. Marriage does not merely protect and nurture children; it is a shield against sexual jealousy, and a unique form of social and economic co-operation, with a mutually supportive division of roles that more than doubles the effectiveness of each partner in their shared bid for security. Marriage fulfils this complex function because it is something more than a contract of mutual co-operation, and something more than an agreement to live together. Hence marriage enjoys – or has until recently enjoyed – a distinct social aura. A wedding is a rite of passage, in which a couple pass from one social condition to another. The ceremony is not the concern of the couple only, but of the entire community that includes them. For this is the way that children are made – made, that is, as new members of society, who will, in their turn, take on the task of social reproduction. Society has a profound interest in marriage, and changes to that institution may alter not merely relations among the living, but also the expectations of those unborn and the legacy of those who predecease them.

Wedding guests, therefore, symbolize the social endorsement of the union that they have assembled to witness, and the marriage is a kind of legitimization of the potentially subversive desire between the partners. Society blesses the union, but only at a price. And the price has been, in traditional Christian societies, a heavy one: sexual fidelity 'till death do us part', and a responsibility for the socializing and educating of the children. As people become more and more reluctant to pay that price, so do weddings become more and more provisional, and the distinction between the socially endorsed union and the merely private arrangement becomes less and less absolute and less and less secure. As sociologists are beginning to observe, however, this gain in freedom for one generation implies a loss for the next. Children born within a marriage are far more likely to be socialized, outgoing and able to form permanent relationships of their own, than children born out of wedlock.[39] For their parents have

---

39 See James Q. Wilson, *The Moral Sense, op. cit.*; Charles Murray, *Losing Ground: American Social Policy 1950–1980, op. cit.*

made a commitment in which the children are included, and of which society approves. This fact is part of the deep phenomenology of the marital home. Children of married parents find a place in society already prepared for them, furnished by a regime of parental sacrifice and protected by social norms. Take away marriage and you expose children to the risk of coming into the world as strangers, a condition in which they may remain for the rest of their lives.

An anthropologist will hardly be surprised, therefore, to discover that marriage is regarded, in most simple societies, as a religious condition. Rites of passage are conducted in the presence of the ancestors, and the ancestors are presided over by the gods. Religion is one way in which the long-term interests of society may animate the short-term decisions of its present members. Hence it is natural that marriage should be seen from within as something divinely ordained, with a sacred aura that reinforces the undertaken duties and elicits the support of the tribe. You don't have to be a religious believer to observe this or to see its point. You need only be aware of what is at stake, when people bring children into the world and claim those children as their own.

Civil Union

The institution of civil marriage is not a modern invention. It was already established under Roman law, which regarded marriage as a distinct legal status, protected and defined by a purely secular jurisdiction. However, the law took note of religious precedent, looked severely on those who departed from its edicts, required a kind of commitment that went well beyond any merely contractual tie involving children and property and held both parties to their obligations. The shadow of religion fell across the Roman marriage ceremony, with its meticulous rituals and sacred words, and the household gods watched over the transition, in which they were intimately concerned. True, Roman marriages were not conceived as eternal unions: they were the legal embodiment of an intention to live monogamously together, and could be ended by noting that the *affectio maritalis* had ceased. Legal recognition that the marriage was over could be obtained without difficulty, and although in later Christian times the Emperor Justinian briefly succeeded in penalizing consensual divorce, it is clear that the Roman law did not regard marriage as a radical existential change.

With the growth of the Papacy marriage was recaptured from the secular powers and reconsecrated as the Church's concern. And so it remained throughout the Middle Ages and the early Renaissance. An uneasy truce was struck between secular jurisdictions and ecclesiastical ceremonies, and the Church's interdiction of divorce ensured that marriage laws would enshrine the idea of a lifelong commitment. Marriage was no longer a complex and rescindable relationship, but a permanent change of status, from which there could be no real return.[40]

When Henry VIII took the English into the Reformation, it was on account of his marital problems. He wanted a divorce and the Church would not grant one. Traditional Catholic teaching holds marriage to be an irreversible change of status, not merely within the community but also before God. Hence a marriage cannot be undone, but only annulled. An annulment does not grant release from an existing marriage but declares that the marriage never was. Naturally enough, the process of annulment has been subject to abuses; but even Henry, Defender of the Faith, could not persuade the Church to take the easy way out of their common problem. When the King took the matter into his own hands it was not in order to break the connection between marriage and the Church. On the contrary, marriage remained Holy Matrimony, and Henry solved the Church's problems by appointing himself as the head of it. It was probably not until the French Revolution that the State declared itself to be the true broker and undoer of marriages, and neither the Catholic nor the Protestant Church has ever accepted this as

---

40 On this point, and the subsequent history of marriage, see John Witte, *From Sacrament to Contract: Marriage, Religion and Law in the Western Tradition*, Louisville, KY: Westminster/John Knox Press, 1997.

doctrine or afforded its comforts to those who view their marriages as purely civil affairs.

Since then, however, we have experienced a steady de-sacralization of the marriage tie. It is not merely that marriage is governed now by a secular law – that has been the case since antiquity. It is that this law is constantly amended, not in order to perpetuate the idea of an existential commitment, but on the contrary to make it possible for commitments to be evaded, and agreements rescinded, by rewriting them as the terms of a contract.

From the external perspective this development must be seen as radical. What was once a socially endorsed change of status has become a private and reversible deal. The social constraints that tied man and wife to each other through all troubles and disharmonies have been one by one removed, to the point where marriage is hardly distinct from a short-term agreement for cohabitation. This has been made more or less explicit in the American case by the pre-nuptial agreement, which specifies a division of property in the event of divorce. Partners now enter the marriage with an escape route already mapped out.

Contracts and Vows

To understand this change we should recognize that, although divorce has been permitted in Protestant cultures for some time, it has not been seen in contractual terms, even by the secular law of marriage. Divorce has been unlike annulment in recognizing that a marriage once existed and is now being undone. But it has been like annulment in recognizing that the spirit of a marriage survives its material death. There could be no return from the state of marriage, but only a transition to another state *beyond* marriage, in which as many of the marital obligations as possible would be salvaged from the ruin and reinstated as lifetime burdens on the parties. Typically, the divorced husband would be charged with the maintenance of his ex-wife, the education and protection of their children and such other liabilities as could be imposed upon a man now faced with a self-made enemy.

With the pre-nuptial agreement, however, divorce takes on a

new meaning. It becomes in a sense the *fulfilment* of the marriage contract, which henceforth loses its force. Spouses no longer enter a marriage but, as it were, stand outside it, fully equipped to move on. Hence marriage has ceased to be what Hegel called a 'substantial tie',[41] and become one of a lifelong series of hand-shakes. Among the wealthy and the sexy serial polygamy is now the norm. But the word 'polygamy' already begs the most impor-tant question – which is whether such an arrangement is really a marriage. Rescindable civil unions cannot conceivably have the function of marriage as traditionally conceived. They cannot guarantee security to children, nor can they summon the willing endorsement of society, by showing the partners' preparedness to make a sacrifice on the future's behalf. The new kind of civil union exists merely to amplify the self-confidence of the partners. Children, neighbours, community, the world – all such others are strangers to the deal. Not surprisingly, when marriage is no more than an official rubber stamp affixed to a purely private contract, people cease to see the point of it. Why bother with the stamp? Whose business is it anyway?

Official policy is, therefore, already recognizing the effect of official policy, which is to downgrade and ultimately abolish the marriage tie. Government forms in Britain ask for details of your 'partner' where once they would have asked for details of your husband or wife. It is all but politically incorrect to declare yourself married to someone (at least to someone of the opposite sex), and many of my liberal friends now refuse to refer to their lifelong companions in terms that imply any greater commitment than that contained in an agreement to share a roof. Children are no longer part of the arrangement, which is conceived purely as a contract between consenting adults. When Kant described marriage as 'a contract for the mutual use of the sexual organs' he may not have had this in mind.[42] But his words were prophetic,

---

41   G. W. F. Hegel, *Philosophy of Right*, tr. T. M. Knox, Oxford: Clarendon Press, 1952, §161.

42   *Kant's Philosophical Correspondence: 1755–99*, ed. and tr. Arnulf Zweig, Chicago 1967, p. 235; *The Metaphysic of Morals*, Academy Ed., p. 277.

and proof of the extent to which his Enlightenment vision was already reshaping the world.

The traditional marriage, seen from the external perspective as a rite of passage to another social condition, is seen from within as a vow. This vow may be preceded by a promise. But it is something more than a promise, since the obligations to which it leads cannot be spelled out in finite terms. A vow of marriage creates an existential tie, not a set of specifiable obligations. And the gradual vanishing of marital vows is one special case of the transition 'from status to contract' which was discussed, from the external perspective, by that great armchair anthropologist Sir Henry Maine.[43] But there is also more to the change than that. The triumph of the contractual view of marriage represents a change in the phenomenology of sexual union, a retreat from the world of 'substantial ties' to a world of negotiated deals. And the world of vows is a world of sacred things, in which holy and indefeasible obligations stand athwart our lives and command us along certain paths, whether we will or not. It is this experience that the Church has always tried to safeguard, and it is one that has been jeopardized by the State, in its efforts to refashion marriage for a secular age.

The Vow of Love

When the Church first declared marriage to be a sacrament, to be administered before the altar in the presence of God, it was attempting to give institutional form to a vow. From the inner perspective, however, this vow preceded the Church's endorsement. And the theory of marriage as a sacrament captures a prior sense that something similar is true of erotic love. Whence does this sense of the sacred arise? Anthropologists can tell us why the vow of love is useful to us, and why it has been selected by our social evolution. But they have no special ability to trace its roots in human experience, or to enable us to understand what happens to the moral life when the vow disappears, and erotic commit-

---

43   Sir Henry Maine, *Ancient Law*, London: John Murray, 1861.

ment is replaced by the sexual handshake. Indeed, anthropologists may be even more tempted than the rest of us, to read their own internal perspective into the behaviour of the people whom they study: witness the now notorious case of Margaret Mead, who travelled all the way to Samoa in order to witness the sexual culture of New York.[44]

The supposed sanctity of the erotic tie, the connection with chastity, celibacy and the vow of love – these themes animated medieval literature, and came to the fore at the time when the ecclesiastical view of marriage as a sacrament was beginning to take a hold on the law and the imagination of medieval Europe. The literature of courtly love, as it came to be known,[45] was an attempt to raise the erotic from the realm of animal passion to that of rational choice. This literature was inspired by neo-Platonist theories which had already exerted considerable influence over Islamic and Hispano-Arabic literature, and which were distilled in the works of Avicenna (Ibn Sinna), the Persian physician and Sufi philosopher who had provided so many of the metaphysical conceptions that shaped the theology of the medieval Church. Much of what is proposed by the poets and philosophers of courtly love is apt to strike us now as absurd. The extraordinary legalism of *Le roman de la rose* and the fictitious 'courts of love' described by Andreas Capellanus and others strikes us now as a vain attempt to deny the obvious truth, which is that sexual desire is not a choice or a judgement but a passion.[46] The medievals were themselves aware of this, and side by side with the courtly literature we find the tales of Tristan and Isolde and Troilus and Cressida, which emphasize the untameable power of sexual longing, and its ability to subvert all that we might erect by way of legal, conventional and institutional restraints.

But it is in these very dramas of passion that we find an explanation for the vow of love and for the aura of sanctity that

---

44 Margaret Mead, *Coming of Age in Samoa*, New York: Morrow, 1928.
45 Actually *l'amour courtois*, so named by Gaston Paris in a seminal article of 1883: 'Lancelot du Lac: *Le Conte de la Charrette*', *Romania* 12, 459–534.
46 Andreas Capellanus, *De arte honesti amandi*, tr. John Jay Parry as *The Art of Courtly Love*, New York: Columbia University Press, 1941.

90   *A Political Philosophy*

surrounds it. The vow is not imposed on lovers by custom, nor required of them by law. It is present in the very experience of desire: such is the burden of the medieval tales. Isolde's desire for Tristan subverts her marriage vows, but only so as to prove that her true vows were not to King Mark but to Tristan. The sin of Cressida is not that she defies the laws of marriage but that she betrays the vow of love that arose in her first desire, and which dedicated her to Troilus.

Well yes, you say, that may have been true of those particular fictions. But what bearing does it have on life as it is lived by the rest of us? We are not heroes of passion, nor given to these catastrophic commitments from which there is no turning back. We are content to live at a lower level, accepting sexual desire as a source of pleasure but wary of the obsessive attachments that it can generate and which leave us perpetually unassuaged.

That response is apt to be supported by a weight of cultural history. It will be said that the vow of love – conceived one way by the courtly literature and another way by the subversive response to it – is in both versions a piece of ideology. It is an attempt to present as a permanent and metaphysical truth what is in fact no more than a passing social fashion, useful in securing the property relations of a vanished leisure class, but with no claim to be the enduring truth of the human condition. The myth of the love-vow had a lasting influence on Western culture, leading to the great celebrations of man-woman love in Shakespeare and Milton, to the heroic passions explored by Racine, to the literature of romantic love and to the operas of Bellini, Verdi and Wagner. But all this is culture, not nature. Other societies have viewed love, desire and marriage in other terms, and the idea of marriage as rooted in a personal choice and an existential commitment is as foreign to oriental traditions as the love of counterpoint, the belief in the Incarnation or a taste for *confit d'oie*.

It is hard to disagree with all that. Yet there is something that it overlooks, something which is at the heart of the medieval conception of the love-vow, and of the marital practices that it has been used to authorize. This thing is the peculiar intentionality of human sexual emotion. Sexual desire is not a desire for sensations. It is a desire for a person: and I mean a *person*, not his or her body, conceived as an object in the physical world, but the person conceived as an incarnate subject, in whom the light of self-consciousness shines and who confronts me eye to eye, and I to I. True desire is also a kind of petition: it demands reciprocity, mutuality and a shared surrender. It is, therefore, compromising, and also threatening. No pursuit of a mere sensation could be compromising or threatening in this way.

Those are not claims about culture, nor are they claims about the way in which desire has been rationalized, idealized or constrained by institutions. They are claims about a particular state of mind, one that only rational beings can experience, and which, nevertheless, has its roots in our embodiment as members of the human species. There are other states of mind that have a passing resemblance to sexual desire, but which do not share its intentionality – for example, the sexual excitement aroused by pornography, or the excitement that finds relief in fetishism and in necrophilia. There is a whole gamut of perversions, the object of which is not to possess another person in a state of mutual surrender but to relieve oneself on a body, to enslave or humiliate, to treat the other as an instrument through which to achieve some sensory excitement, and so on. But in calling these things perversions we indicate a defect in the intentionality from which they spring. They are no more to be seen as expressions of sexual desire than the desire to eat your child is to be seen as an expression of love, even when love, of a perverted kind, is the cause of it. Such is the complexity of the human condition that the mental forces that erupt in us can find just such peculiar outlets. But in describing them as perversions we convey the idea that a state of mind has a normal object, a normal fulfilment and a normal course towards its goal. In the case of sexual desire the norm can be seen externally, in terms of its social function, and also internally, as a feature of the intentional object and of the description under which he or she is desired.

Postmodern Sex

Now many people will question what I have said about desire. There is a picture of human sexuality that is propagated by the media, by popular culture and by much sex education in our schools, which tries both to discount the differences between us and the other animals, and also to remove every hint of the forbidden, the dangerous and the sacred. It is a picture that makes no place for shame, save as a lingering disability, and which describes the experience of sex as a kind of bodily sensation. Sexual initiation, according to this picture, means learning to overcome guilt and shame, to put aside our hesitations and to enjoy what is described in the literature as 'good sex'. The function of sex education in schools – and especially in those schools controlled by the State – is to rescue children from the commitments that have been attached to desire by displaying sex as a matter of cost-free pleasure. Even to describe desire as I have done in the foregoing paragraphs is regarded, by many educationists, as an offence – a way of cluttering the minds of children with unmanageable guilt. Such educationists regard the free play of sexual titillation as a far healthier option than the death-encompassing passions associated with the old conception of erotic love.[47] Most parents, however, encountering this attitude to sex and the literature used to implant it in the adolescent mind, experience a surge of revulsion, even going so far as to question the right of the State so to poison the hearts of their children. Indeed, sex education has become one of the principal battlegrounds between the family and the State. There is a reason for this, to which I return.

Before the advent of modern sex education, the object of desire was represented through concepts of purity and pollution,

---

47 The research necessary to back up these claims (at least in the case of England and Wales) is available in Valerie Riches, *Sex Education or Indoctrination: how ideology has triumphed over facts*, with additional research by Norman Wells, London: Family and Youth Concern, 2004. Americans will be familiar with the research of Kay Hymowitz and others to the same effect.

sanctity and desecration, and it is the transition between these states that is dramatized in the story of Troilus and Cressida. It is because the object of desire has been perceived in this way that jealousy can take the murderous form in human beings that Shakespeare puts before us in *Othello*. Desdemona, in Othello's eyes, has been ransacked, polluted, like a violated temple, and only her death can extinguish this sacrilege and restore the pre-existing holiness. What Shakespeare is describing here is precisely not a local form of erotic passion, but a human universal, a predicament that we are involved in by the very fact of sexual desire. That sexual desire is directed towards an existential commitment is the unwritten assumption of the literature of erotic love, from *Daphnis and Chloë* to the puppet plays of Chikamatsu, and from *Aucassin et Nicolette* to *Lady Chatterley's Lover*.

This existential aspect of desire makes it dangerous. Rape is a crime not because it involves force, but because it is a desecration, a spoiling and polluting of that which it is in a woman's nature to hold in reserve until it can be given freely. If sexual desire were merely the desire for sexual sensations, this ransacking of the body could not occur: to be raped would then be no worse than to be spat upon. It is precisely the existential seizure that humiliates and destroys. For it is a kind of murder, a reducing of the embodied person to a corpse.

Again, however, we must confront the modern sceptic. Even if people once understood the sexual act through those quasi-religious conceptions, the sceptic will argue, they do so no longer. There is now neither pollution nor taboo, but an easygoing market in sexual commodities: a market which can be entered without shame and left without damage. And maybe the growth of this market, and its extension, through sex education, to an ever-growing number of participants, is a real contribution to human freedom and to the undistinguished contentment of the postmodern herd.

It seems to me, however, that desire freed from moral constraints, and from the ethic of pollution and taboo, is a new and highly artificial state of mind. It can be maintained in being only

by forms of discourse that wilfully disenchant the sexual act and
the human body: in other words, which are wilfully obscene. This
partly explains the gradual invasion of popular culture by explicit
sexual images, and the consequent shift in focus from the human
subject to the dehumanized object. These cultural developments
are not random: they have a function, and this function can be
clearly seen when we contrast the old Hollywood approach to
romance with the modern cult of explicit images.

When the erotic kiss first became obligatory on the cinema
screen it was construed as a coming together of faces, each fully
personalized through dialogue. The two faces had carried the
burden of a developing drama, and were inseparable in thought
from the individuals whose faces they were. When, in the last
seconds of the Hollywood movie, the faces tremblingly
approached each other, to be clichéd together in a clinch, the
characters sank away from us into their mutual desire. This desire
was their own affair, a kind of avenue out of the story, that took
them quickly off the screen and into marriage.

Pornography is the opposite of that: the face is more or less
ignored, and in any case is endowed with no personality and
made party to no human dialogue. Only the sexual organs,
construed not as agents but as patients, or rather impatients,
carry the burden of contact. Sexual organs, unlike faces, can be
treated as instruments; they are rival means to the common end of
friction, and therefore essentially substitutable. Pornography
refocuses desire, not on the other who is desired, but on the
sexual act itself, viewed as a meeting of bodies. The intentionality
of the sexual act, conceived in this disenchanted way, is radically
changed. It ceases to be an expression of interpersonal longing,
still less of the desire to hold, to possess, to be filled with love. It
becomes a kind of sacrilege – a wiping away of freedom, personality and transcendence, to reveal the passionless contortions of
what is merely flesh. Pornography is, therefore, functional in
relation to a society of uncommitted partnerships. It serves to
desecrate and thereby neutralize our sense that the object of desire
is made sacred and irreplaceable by our longing. By shifting the
focus downwards, from the end to the means, from the subject to

the object, pornography diverts sexual feeling away from its normal course, which is commitment, and empties it of its existential seriousness. Pornography is sex education for life, as it were.

State and Family

To what point does this bring us, in the contemporary discussions over marriage? My tentative conclusion is this: that the view of marriage as a sacrament is an accurate, if theologically loaded, account of how marriage has been experienced, of why it is wanted and of what it inwardly does to those who enter it. Marriage is not a contract of cohabitation, but a vow of togetherness. Its foundation is erotic, not in the sense that all marriages begin in or exist through desire, but in the sense that, without desire, the institution would rest on nothing in the human condition. At the same time, looked at from outside, with the eye of the anthropologist, marriage has a function, which is to ensure social reproduction, the socializing of children and the passing on of social capital. Without marriage it is doubtful that those processes would occur, but when they occur they provide both a fulfilment of sexual union and a way to transcend its scant imperatives, into a realm of duty, love and pride. The inner, sacramental, character of marriage is therefore reinforced by its external function. Together they endow marriage with its distinctive character, as an institution that is normal and sublime in equal measure.

When the State usurped the rite of matrimony, and reshaped what had once been holy law, it was inevitable that it should loosen the marital tie. For the State does not represent the Eternal, nor does it have so much regard for future generations that it can disregard the whims of the merely living. The State is always and inevitably the instrument of its current members; it will respond to their pressures and try to satisfy their demands. It has, therefore, found it expedient to undo the sacrament, to permit easy divorce, to reduce marriage from a vow to a contract and – in the most recent act of liberalization – to permit marriage, or its civil 'equivalent', between people of the same sex. None of this has been done with evil motives, and always there has been, in the back of people's minds, a memory of the sacred and existential ties that distinguish people from animals and enduring societies from madding crowds. The desire has been to retain the distinctiveness of marriage, as the best that we can hope for by way of a lasting commitment, while escaping from its more onerous demands – demands that people are no longer prepared to recognize. As a result marriage has ceased to be a rite of passage into another and higher life, and become a bureaucratic stamp, with which to endorse our temporary choices. I would not call this a gain in freedom – for those choices have never been denied to us, and by dignifying them with the name of marriage we merely place another obstacle before the option to which humanity has devoted so much of its idealizing fervour. Of course, we are still free to dedicate our lives to each other, to our home and to our children. But this act is rendered the more difficult, the less society recognizes the uniqueness, the value and the sacrificial character of what we do. Just as people are less disposed to assume the burdens of high office when society withholds the dignities and privileges which those offices have previously signified, so are they less disposed to enter real marriages, when society acknowledges no distinction between marriages that deserve the name, and relationships that merely borrow the title.

Ordinary conjugal people, who marry and raise children in the traditional way, and who believe that these acts point beyond the present moment to an indefinite future and a transcendental law, have a voice in law-making, and will tend to vote for legislators who uphold the sacramental view of marriage and who pass laws endorsing the normal way of marital sacrifice. From the external point of view, that is what an anthropologist would expect. For societies endure only when they are devoted to future generations, and collapse like the Roman Empire when the pleasures and fancies of the living consume the stock of social capital. In the United States, however, there is another way to legislation, through the Supreme Court, and this way is the way of the State and of the elites who control it. And because the US Supreme Court can override any merely democratically elected body, and will – as the case of *Roe v. Wade* amply demonstrates – use any measure of sophistical argument if it sees the need to do so, Americans are increasingly aware that – in many of the most important matters, the matters that govern the life and death of society – it is the State, not the people, that decides. The attitude of the State to marriage should, therefore, be set beside its attitude to sex education and the bearing of children. The burden of state-sponsored sex education, I have suggested, is to turn the sexual urge away from erotic passion, marital commitment and child-bearing, towards disposable pleasures. This attitude is reinforced by the State's support for abortion, and its 'discovery', in *Roe v. Wade*, that the unborn have no rights under the Constitution and therefore no rights at all. Put all this together with the State's constant tendency to erode the tie of marriage, and you will be tempted to believe that the State has set itself against the goal of reproduction. This has not been a conscious decision. Nevertheless, it reflects a vast movement in the modern world, towards the confiscation of hereditary rights.

Some will see this attitude as involving a kind of collective infanticide: such, I suspect, is the response of the Roman Catholic Church. Others, however, welcome it, even under the somewhat bleak description that I have offered. Thus Richard Rorty, in *Achieving Our Country*, ostensibly a critique of the anti-patriotism of the left establishment, sees the emergence of the easygoing culture of promiscuity, and the political correctness which is well on the way to censoring out every alternative, as positive steps towards the principal thing that matters, which is an 'Enlightenment utopia' in which complete equality of condition will have at last been achieved.[48] To get there you need the Supreme Court, if only to extinguish those exclusive passions and loyalties that are the source of local privilege. The fact that the resulting Utopia will be unable to reproduce itself is not a fact that pragmatists like

---

48 Richard Rorty, *Achieving Our Country: Leftist Thought in Twentieth Century America*, New York: Routledge, 2002.

Rorty are equipped to notice. And what a pragmatist doesn't notice is in any case not a fact.[49]

The Function of Ideology

It is here that we should step back from the discussion of marriage in order to revisit the Marxist distinction between ideology and science. A scientific theory is part of our search for truth, and it endures because it has not been refuted. An ideology is part of our search for stability, and it endures because it fulfils a social function, shoring up customs, practices and institutions that require just this if they are to provide their benefits. We can see the point from the initial example that I took of seasonal warfare. The warrior's belief that this is a sacred duty, an obligation to the ancestors and a solemn gesture of brotherhood is ideological. His belief is to be explained in terms of its function, rather than its explanatory power. Its function, roughly, is to commit the warrior to his dangerous exploits, in a way that he could be committed by no merely dispassionate analysis of the cost and benefit of pursuing them. From the external point of view seasonal warfare too must be explained by its function: it is a way of securing territory, controlling populations and achieving equilibrium in the search for scarce resources. The external view is scientific: it explains the behaviour of the tribe but does not justify it. The internal view is ideological: it justifies the behaviour but does not explain it. The true explanation of the behaviour is also an explanation of the ideology, and in both cases the explanation refers to a social function.

You might wish to apply Marx's distinction to what I have said about sex and marriage. The external viewpoint offers an explanation of marriage, in terms of its social function. It is because it

49 Still, it is worth pointing out that societies where marriage has broken down or where children are routinely born out of wedlock are now dying: in Europe this happens because the children are not born, in sub-Saharan Africa because the children die of AIDS. In societies where marriage is the norm and children are born in wedlock, population is increasing, notably in the Islamic world.

facilitates social reproduction that marriage exists and endures. If marriage became dysfunctional it would disappear, just as seasonal warfare has disappeared from modern societies. This external explanation can also form the starting point for a justification, by showing that the consequences attached to marriage are socially beneficial, and the consequences of destroying marriage socially disastrous. I belief that this kind of consequentialist justification of marriage has already been made by Charles Murray, James Q. Wilson and others. However, there is also an internal justification of marriage, in terms of the vector towards commitment that is contained within erotic passion. The Marxian anthropologist might say of this internal justification that it is 'mere ideology', meaning that it is to be explained in terms of its function, in securing marital commitment, but has no rational basis in the erotic tie itself. To explain the institution of marriage from the external perspective is also to expose the internal perspective as a kind of illusion, which records no independent fact of the matter, being merely an aura cast by the institution in the minds of those over whom it holds sway.

Although not all debunkers of 'bourgeois' society make use of Marx's distinction between ideology and science, the idea that our dearest beliefs and most precious values are merely ideological constructs, destined to disappear with the institutions and the power relations that temporarily require them, is now a common assumption in the social science and humanities departments of our universities. It tells us that the view of marriage as a sacrament and the associated experience of erotic love as involving a vow, a commitment and an existential tie are all part of the ideology of marriage. When marriage loses its function so too does the ideology; and since the ideology rests on no independent ground, it will disappear like a dream in the waking conditions of modernity. Moreover, the follower of Michel Foucault will say, societies no longer require bourgeois marriage in order to generate children and endow them with social capital. On the contrary, bourgeois marriage stands in the way of the new forms of social reproduction, which are all in the hands of the State. Through welfare benefits and social initiatives the State takes charge not only of the education of children but also of their production. Modern sex education is not concerned to convey the facts about sex any more than was the old apprenticeship in chastity. Sex education too is ideology, functional in relation to the new form of social reproduction, in which the parties are the single mother and the State, and in which exclusive and lifelong attachments threaten the State's control over the reproductive process. By de-sacralizing the sexual bond, and removing the existential danger, the new ideology prepares the way for a process of social reproduction in which sexual desire and sexual excitement play only a transitory and non-constitutive part.

My response to that argument is twofold. Although (as I suggested above) modern sex education is functional in relation to the society that it seems to produce, I do not believe that the function of traditional marriage can be effectively performed by the Welfare State or by any other institution in which love is not the principal foundation. Empirical observation is beginning to confirm what should have been obvious *a priori*, which is that societies in which the vow of marriage is giving way to the contract for sexual pleasure are also rapidly ceasing to reproduce themselves.

Second, and more importantly, the theory of ideology is incomplete, and depends on a contrast, between the merely functional and the scientific, that is neither exhaustive nor exclusive. The belief that murder is wrong is not a scientific belief: it is not based on evidence nor can it be refuted. No society could survive without this belief, and in that sense it serves a social function. But it is also true, objective, capable – we all assume – of justification. And if the justification is hard to find, that does not distinguish the belief that murder is wrong from the belief that two plus two is four.

Similarly, our beliefs about the bindingness of erotic love and the existential change that it inflicts on us are objective, based in a true apprehension of what is at stake in our sexual adventures, and what is needed for our fulfilment. To spell out the justification may be hard, and the full reality of sexual emotion will always be more readily presented by a work of art, such as

Troilus and Criseyde, *Tristan und Isolde* or *Mansfield Park* than by a metaphysical discourse. Nevertheless, it is true of erotic feelings as it is of moral values, that their functionality does not undermine the vision that they impart, and that this vision is also a validation.

Gay Marriage

Heterosexual union is imbued with the sense that your partner's sexual nature is strange to you, a territory into which you intrude without prior knowledge and in which the other and not the self is the only reliable guide. This experience has profound repercussions for our sense of the danger and the mystery of sexual union, and these repercussions are surely part of what people have had in mind in clothing marriage as a sacrament, and the ceremony of marriage as a rite of passage from one form of safety to another. Traditional marriage was not only a rite of passage from adolescence to adulthood; nor was it only a way of endorsing and guaranteeing the raising of children. It was also a dramatization of sexual difference. Marriage kept the sexes at such a distance from each other that their coming together became an existential leap, rather than a passing experiment. The intentionality of desire was shaped by this, and even if the shaping was – at some deep level – a cultural and not a human universal, it endowed desire with its intrinsic nuptiality, and marriage with its transformatory goal. To regard gay marriage as simply another option within the institution is to ignore the fact that an institution shapes the motive for joining it. Marriage has grown around the idea of sexual difference and all that sexual difference means. To make this feature accidental rather than essential is to change marriage beyond recognition. Gays want marriage because they want the social endorsement that it signifies; but by admitting gay marriage we deprive marriage of its social meaning, as the blessing conferred by the unborn on the living. The pressure for gay marriage is, therefore, in a certain measure self-defeating. It resembles Henry VIII's move to gain ecclesiastical endorsement for his divorce, by making himself head of the Church. The Church that endorsed his divorce thereby ceased to be the Church whose endorsement he was seeking.

That does not alter the fact that gay marriage furthers the hidden tendency of the postmodern State, which is to rewrite all commitments as contracts between the living. It is a near certainty, therefore, that the American State, acting through the Supreme Court, will 'discover' a constitutional right to gay marriage just as it discovered constitutional rights to abortion and pornography, and just as it will discover, when asked, a right to no-fault divorce.

Those who are troubled by this, and who wish to register their protest, will have to struggle against powerful forms of censorship. People who dissent from what is fast becoming orthodoxy in the matter of 'gay rights' are now routinely accused of 'homophobia'. All over America there are appointment committees intent on examining candidates for suspected homophobia and summarily dismissing them once the accusation has been made: 'You can't have that woman pleading at the Bar, she is a Christian fundamentalist and a homophobe'; 'No, even if he is the world's authority on second dynasty hieroglyphs, you can't give him tenure, after that homophobic outburst last Friday'. This censorship will advance the cause of those who have made it their business to 'normalize' the idea of homosexual union. It will not be possible to resist it, any more than it has proved possible to resist the feminist censorship of the truth about sexual difference. But maybe it will be possible to entertain, between consenting adults in private, the thought that homosexual marriage is really no such thing.[50]

---

50 I have benefited greatly from Seana Sugrue's comments on an earlier draft of this chapter.

6

Extinguishing the Light

The seismic waves from May 1968 shook the ground beneath the frail battlements of high culture and caused citadel after citadel to fall. Thinkers who had obtained prominence in the year of the Parisian barricades were crowned with a halo of rectitude that no preacher of Anglo-Saxon common sense could possibly earn. Quite suddenly, without anyone really discussing it, the university curriculum in the humanities was dominated by Althusser, Foucault, Barthes and, shortly afterwards, by Derrida, Kristeva and other writers for the journal *Tel Quel*.

This overnight conquest was something entirely unusual in the world of ideas. To the sceptical observer it suggested that the new thinkers were being adopted for reasons other than the power of their arguments or the truth of their views. I recall the labour with which, over several weeks of intense application, we had studied Wittgenstein's *Philosophical Investigations*, and the joy that flooded us as the private language argument finally made sense. The same experience was granted with reading Leavis's essay on reality and sincerity in poetry, in which an argument equally subtle and all the more vivid for being focused on concrete examples, suddenly dawned on us, and its implications shot like rays of cheerful sunlight to the furthest reaches of our minds.

Those intellectual experiences were not morally neutral. The Leavisite vision of literature, and the Wittgensteinian conception of mind and language, were the vanguards, for me, of a long train of self-examination and critical reflection, in which many dear illusions had to be jettisoned and many values rethought. That is what humane education amounted to: the intellectual revision of the moral landscape. At the same time, however, they were not conversion experiences, such as form the heart of evangelical religions. I did not come away from Wittgenstein or Leavis with a sense of moral rebirth or spiritual mission, nor did I lose, through reading them, the guilt of my transgressions or the desire to make amends for them. The effect of reading those thinkers was comparable to the joy we had experienced at school, when studying Piaggio's *Differential Equations*, and we stood in wonder at the edge of real mathematics, seeing its shining citadel of pure reasoning rise above us, inaccessible, awe-inspiring, yet indisputably real. After that experience it was impossible to doubt the credentials of mathematics as a source of objective knowledge and a model of proof, just as it was impossible to doubt that philosophy in the spirit of Wittgenstein or criticism in that of Leavis were forms of rational argument, with real results that bore on the nature and meaning of life in this world.

When the advocates of the French avant-garde burst on the scene it was with a weapon called 'structuralism', which they wielded against the old authorities in full confidence of victory. The charm of this weapon was that, while brandished in front of the enemy, it miraculously stabbed him in the back. Those politically neutral and impartial conceptions by which we had set such store were not refuted – refutation was no longer necessary. By 'decoding' the old authorities the structuralist purported to show that they are not neutral or impartial at all, but every bit as political as the 'theories' that challenge them, and all the more pernicious for hiding their ideology in a carapace of reasoned argument. By decoding the arguments of Wittgenstein and Leavis you could discover the concealed assumptions on which they depend, and for which they could offer no defence. And the assumptions are those of a bourgeois culture that had lost any claim to our involvement.

The subversive agenda remained in place as the authorities changed. In the manner of scholastic theology, the structuralists gave way to the 'post-structuralists', who were soon ousted by 'deconstruction', itself to be absorbed into a general 'postmodernist' perspective which promoted itself as 'beyond theory', while claiming the right, nevertheless, to undermine every procedure that conflicted with its agenda-driven view of scholarship. Postmodernism became the general term for academic writing that recognized the 'postmodern condition' and the 'end of ideology'. How you define the postmodern condition depends on how you define modernity. But the question of definition became urgent only in the late 1970s, for a curious reason that should be borne in mind when reading the French exponents of the idea, such as Jean Baudrillard and Jean-François Lyotard.

The reason is this: recent French literary culture has been largely built around one of the projects of modernity: the revolt against bourgeois norms, in the name of aesthetic licence. In Sartre and Foucault, in Barthes and Lacan, in the writers for *Tel Quel* (including Kristeva and Derrida), in sociologists like Bourdieu, even in composers like Boulez and Barraqué, you find the same cultural and intellectual agenda – which is the repudiation of bourgeois respectability and the Catholic culture of France. This, combined with *nostalgie de la boue*, a residue of romantic diabolism and a long flirtation with Marxism and the Communist Party, created the unique culture of Paris in the 1960s, to which people like Baudrillard and Lyotard belonged. When their former worldview became manifestly untenable those two thinkers set themselves the task of marketing the postmodern condition in its stead.

Thus, in *The Postmodern Condition* – a 'report on knowledge', prepared, curiously enough, for the government of Quebec in 1979 – Lyotard tells us that the old projects of modernity have collapsed, since they have lost the 'metanarratives' through which they were 'legitimized'. In particular, the story that the French intellectuals told themselves – namely, that there was a path out of bourgeois reality through the written word – was a lie. There is no such thing as the emancipation of mankind from bourgeois normality; no such thing as a victory over consumerism or gadgets or 'instrumental reasoning'; no such thing as a release from laws and property and institutions into the transcendental playgroup. Or rather, if there is such a thing, it is not what we were looking for, being as desolate and imprisoning as the routines we must discard in attaining it. The great 'metanarratives' of emancipation can no longer be believed.

Those modernist narratives had pointed fowards to a future state, unlike the backward-looking narratives (the myths and the religions) which legitimize traditional societies. And the future state – the Idea to be realized (freedom, enlightenment, socialism, prosperity, progress) – has 'legitimating value' because it is universal. The narratives of modernity are cosmopolitan, in Kant's sense: they are promises made to all mankind.

There is something right about that, and also about the suggestion that the narratives are no longer believable. And we should be grateful for this. For if you look back at the 2 million dead of the French Revolution, at the 60 million dead in obedience to Lenin and Stalin, at the comparable achievements of Sartre's hero Mao and his disciple Pol Pot, you will see just what this modern 'legitimacy' has meant. That was what Burke perceived, as did his many conservative successors, from Coleridge to Maitland, from de Maistre to Simone Weil and from Hegel to Gierke, whose backward-looking narratives were not, as Lyotard would have us believe, merely myths, but accounts of law, tradition and custom – in other words, of the only known salves for the wounds of social conflict. In fact Lyotard has a sneaking attachment to the narratives of modernity, and cunningly shifts the blame for the modernist crimes to various anti-modern or *völkisch* tendencies, like Jacobinism (for so he sees it) and Nazism. When the opportunity arises to express his anti-capitalist and anti-bourgeois sentiment he seizes it; and the eventual picture of modernity is one of a heroic project that must be abandoned, not in order to reassume the responsibilities that were cast off as we left the premodern age, but in order to escape from these and all other burdens. Postmodernism turns out to be simply the latest venture of the 'culture of repudiation' that leapt on to the stage of history in 1968.

It is in terms of this culture that we should understand both the conversion experience of the new curriculum, and the underlying orthodoxy to which it tends. The ruling postmodernist idea is that Western culture is a burden from which we have now been released. And the release is total. All constraints on the mind, including the discredited rules of truth, objectivity and meaning, have withered away. With the collapse of the old culture we confront a denuded mindscape, without values, goals or meaning, and the postmodern curriculum is designed to show this. Hence the need for a new critical language – a language in which syntax is all, and semantics no more than a memory. Here, in a sentence from Gayatri Chakravorty Spivak, is an instance:

> The rememoration of the 'present' as space is the possibility of the utopian imperative of no-(particular)-place, the metropolitan project that can supplement the post-colonial attempt at the impossible cathexis of place-bound history as the lost time of the spectator.[51]

Whatever that sentence is about, it is clearly no laughing matter. The style is one of po-faced, or pomo-faced, seriousness, not without a certain air of menace. The ability of writers like Alan Sokal[52] to laugh at such utterances is matched by the total inability of their authors to laugh at anything. Literary 'theory' is a joke-free zone, and never more humourless than when pretending, as Jacques Derrida sometimes pretended, that it is all a joke. For laughter, like irony, is a kind of acceptance. In the normal run of things to laugh is to forgive, since what we see as absurd no longer threatens us. Postmodernist theory, however, is not prepared to forgive its target for anything whatsoever.

Spivak's sentence is not exactly meaningless; but the meaning shines through the greyness of the prose like a fire burning beyond it. To understand it you must look for clues: for instance, there is the reference to a Utopian imperative, a metropolitan project, which is part of a post-colonial attempt. Words like

---

51   'Psychoanalysis in Left Field and Fieldworking: Examples to Fit the Title', in *Speculations after Freud: Psychoanalysis, Philosophy and Culture*, eds Sonu Shamdasani and Michael Münchow, London and New York: Routledge, 1994, p. 63.
52   Alan Sokal and Jean Bricmont, *Intellectual Impostures: Postmodern Philosophers' Abuse of Science*, London: Profile Books, 1998.

'imperative', 'project' and 'attempt' all indicate a call to action. Invented words ('rememoration'), out-of-place technicalities ('cathexis', echoing Strachey's mistranslation of Freud), unexplained quotation marks ('present') and parentheses ('no-(particular)-place') and references to abstractions, such as space and time, serve to neutralize the normal process of meaning. But through the clues – words like 'utopia' and 'post-colonial' – you can arrive at the gist. And the gist is opposition. This writer is setting herself and her readers against the 'colonial' world, favouring a new Utopia that will rearrange the social and cultural landscape of modern society and also deprive the old culture of its grip.

Alan Sokal and Jean Bricmont suggest that this gobbledygook does a disservice to the broadly left-wing and progressive causes with which it is associated. To emphasize the point they refer to their own left-wing beliefs, and to their conviction that clarity, objectivity and genuine science are the real weapons to be used in the fight for social justice. This sentiment is echoed by Barbara Epstein, who both deplores the association of postmodern theorizing with the left and applauds the emergence of humanities departments and faculties which are overtly committed to left-wing and progressive causes.[53] She sees postmodern theory as a profoundly retrogressive development, which prevents the academic left from seizing the intellectual high ground in the battle of ideas.

Against that, I would suggest that gobbledygook is far more effective in propagating left-wing and progressive opinions than reasoned argument, for the simple reason that progressive opinions, once explicitly stated, expose themselves to the threat of refutation, something that they do not always survive. The purpose of the jargon is not to find novel reasons for the posture of cultural opposition, but to render that posture impregnable, by putting it beyond rational debate. The many 'methods' of the postmodernist curriculum have one thing in common, which is that they do not argue for their political posture but assume it,

---

53   'Postmodernism and the Left', *New Politics*, Winter 1997.

and at the same time conceal that assumption deep within a protective carapace of nonsense. In this respect they are theological, rather than scientific, theories: theories designed not to establish some belief but to protect that belief from rational criticism.

Gresham's law, which tells us that bad money drives out good, has a simple explanation, namely that people, knowing the worth of good money, hoard it, and circulate the counterfeit money in its stead. This law ought not to operate in the intellectual world. Good theories ought to drive out bad, since good theories are those that survive refutation, and sense ought to drive out nonsense, since nonsense has nothing to say. In the humanities, however, a kind of Gresham's law seems to hold: bad theories drive out good, and nonsense drives out sense. Various explanations have been offered for this,[54] some more plausible than others. The important point is that the survival of a literary theory depends not on its remaining unrefuted, but on its ability to make refutation undesirable, impossible or both. Refutation is undesirable when the theory is so bound up with some approved political posture as to be almost indistinguishable from it, and impossible when the theory is surrounded by an impenetrable wall of nonsense. Hence new literary theories come quickly to dominate academic discourse, and the reader is deprived of the currency in which to offer his dissent. There is no way of formulating, in the jargon of Queer Theory, Discourse Theory, Deconstruction, etc., the elementary beliefs about the human condition which form the bedrock of traditional cultures: beliefs about the deep differences and affinities between men and women, about the naturalness of the family, about the religious need and transcendental longing of our species.

But this brings me to another feature of the new methods in the humanities, which is the shared, though often covert, adoption of a perspectival viewpoint. Nietzsche's celebrated announcement

---

54　See, for example, R. A. D. Grant, 'On Deconstruction' in *Imagining the Real*, London: Macmillan, 2004; Roger Scruton, *An Intelligent Person's Guide to Modern Culture*, South Bend, IN: St Augustine's Press, 2000, chs 11 and 12.

that there are no truths but only interpretations, is reaffirmed in a thousand different ways by the new forms of scholarship, and although Nietzsche's utterance is blatantly paradoxical, since it can be true only if it isn't, the paradox is once again concealed within the postmodern jargon. This perspectivalism appears in many forms, and is often dressed up as something highly original. For example there is Foucault's theory that truths are never simply truths but rather part of the *episteme* of an epoch, the *episteme* belonging to the ruling 'discourse'. Opposition between doctrines is, at the deeper level, a contest between the powers that require them: the important thing in any intellectual dispute, therefore, is to be on the side of the liberator against the oppressor. Likewise there is the notion, common to American feminists like Judith Butler and Andrea Dworkin, that 'gender' and 'sexuality' are social constructs, which can be differently constructed for different purposes and with different political goals. There is no objective fact of the matter about sex or gender, simply competing political projects, each attempting to construct the sexes in its own favoured way.

Again the notorious pronouncement of Luce Irigaray that $E = mc^2$ is a 'sexed equation' which 'privileges the speed of light over other speeds that are vitally necessary to us', and which therefore belongs to the 'masculine physics' that 'privileges' rigid over fluid entities, conveys the same perspectival assumption.[55] There is no objective truth in the matter: merely contrasting perspectives, one masculine, another feminine, in competition for the capture of political space. If we ask ourselves why Richard Rorty has become such an authority in the postmodern academy it must surely be because he is one of the few respected philosophers[56] who takes this perspectivalism seriously. Rorty's pragmatism

55   'Sujet de la science, sujet sexué?', in *Sens et place des connaissances dan la société: 3ème confrontation*, Paris: CNRS, 1987, p. 110.
56   Not the only one, however. There are also the equally influential Thomas Kuhn, of *The Structure of Scientific Revolutions* (second edn), Chicago: University of Chicago Press, 1970, and Paul Feyerabend, of *Against Method* (third edn), London: Verso, 1993, both effectively demolished in Sokal and Bricmont, *op. cit.*

seems to imply that the contest between competing views is always in the end a contest of power, that there is no truth independent of the interests of those struggling to capture it, and that if feminists are empowered by the belief that women are in every respect the equals of men then they are entitled to that belief, as much as to the belief that $2 + 2 = 4$ – or maybe to the even more empowering belief that $2 + 2 = 5$.

This perspectivalism appeals to students far more than any of the gibberish used to advance it. For it corresponds to their own deep disorientation, as they enter university with all their old certainties in disarray, and find themselves confronted on every side by a determined assault on the values and beliefs that their parents had wished to implant in them. It is a natural response for young people to retreat from conviction when conviction gives offence. A posture of total relativism recommends itself, since it leaves every belief, and every value, free-floating and foundation-less. In these circumstances we can all agree, since we are agreeing about nothing. Rival worldviews are merely rival flavours imparted to the same diet of doubts.

According to the postmodernist, the old curriculum is designed to induce adherence to the underlying assumptions of Western culture, assumptions that it does not put in question since they are the unspoken premises of its worldview. The claims to impartiality, objectivity and educational standards are just as much part of the mask as the curriculum itself. It may be that conservatives, liberals and socialists can all imbibe this 'impartial' knowledge; but they do so by closing their minds to the real alternatives. Their separate political postures are simply adjoining enclaves within a common territory, and the effect of their education is to prevent them from thinking outside that territory or questioning the scheme of values that prevails within it. Which is to say that the old curriculum is just as political, in its way, as the new one, and additionally pernicious on account of the pretence that it is no such thing.

If a culture were merely a collection of beliefs to be accepted, texts to be studied, works of art to be absorbed, then it would be hard to explain the animus of the new curriculum towards the old. Once we see culture for what it is, however, this animus becomes comprehensible. A culture is a form of membership, and the high culture that is its self-conscious part perpetuates the memory of that membership and exalts it into something natural, unchangeable and serene. When religious faith declines it becomes difficult for intellectuals to believe that they really belong to the same community as ordinary people. Their claims to priesthood have been exploded, and their isolation in academies sets them at an impassable distance from those whose idea of adventure is to go out and mow the lawn. Confronted with a class of adolescents, and aware of the impossibility of joining the culture from which those adolescents have emerged, the teacher makes a bid for a new form of membership based in the systematic rejection of the old. The emergence of a culture of repudiation is, therefore, a normal result of the breakdown of an old religion. Faced everywhere by customs, artefacts and rituals that have been shorn of their old authority, the would-be priest is moved to acts of sacrilege and iconoclasm.

The remedy for this state of mind is Enlightenment, which endows the intellectual with a new and redemptive role. Instead of submitting to the demands of religion, enlightened intellectuals devote themselves to truth in general, and the truth about the human world in particular. Enlightenment means distinguishing habits that stifle our potential from habits that fulfil it, exploring the ways in which our culture promotes and frustrates our happiness, and the ways in which it aids or impedes the reproduction of a viable society.

Enlightenment, so defined, has for centuries been intrinsic to Western culture, which has grown and altered in the light of its own self-examination. The most striking feature of the postmodernist curriculum however, lies in its explicit rejection of Enlightenment, its disposition to treat reason as a parochial concern of Western culture and to place 'truth', 'objectivity' and 'impartial judgement' in inverted commas. Richard Rorty's 'pragmatism' has been influential because it is conceived as the ultimate rationalization of those inverted commas: reason's final adoption of the irrational as the only available antidote to its own congenital solitude.

Crudely put, pragmatism is the view that 'true' means useful. The most useful belief is the one that gives me the best handle on the world: the belief which, when acted upon, holds out the greatest prospect of success. Obviously, that is not a sufficient characterization of the difference between the true and the false. Anyone seeking a career in an American university will find feminist beliefs useful, just as racist beliefs were useful to the university apparatchik in Nazi Germany. But this hardly shows those beliefs to be true. So what do we *really* mean by 'useful'? One suggestion is this: a belief is useful when it is part of a successful theory. But a successful theory is one that makes true predictions. Hence we have gone round in a circle, defining truth by utility and utility by truth. Indeed, it is hard to find a plausible pragmatism that does not come down to this: that a true proposition is one that is useful in the way that *true* propositions are useful. Impeccable, but vacuous.

Rorty eschews the old and respectable pragmatism of Peirce, Dewey and Quine, who attempted to reconcile theory with practice, and truth with success. For him 'pragmatism' is another name for the postmodernist project, which consists in the search for a community beyond Enlightenment, a community that has relinquished truth and objectivity altogether. As he puts it:

> Pragmatists view truth as . . . what is good for *us* to believe. . . . They see the gap between truth and justification not as something to be bridged by isolating a natural and transcultural sort of rationality which can be used to criticise certain cultures and praise others, but simply as the gap between the actual good and the possible better. . . . For pragmatists, the desire for objectivity is not the desire to escape the limitations of one's community, but simply the desire for as much intersubjective agreement as possible, the desire to extend the reference of 'us' as far as we can.[57]

---

57 *Objectivity, Realism and Truth*, Cambridge: CUP, 1991, pp. 22–3.

In other words, pragmatism enables us to dismiss the idea of a 'trans-cultural . . . rationality'. There is no point to the old ideas of objectivity and universal truth; all that matters is the fact that *we* agree. But who are we? And what do we agree about? Turn to Rorty's essays, and you discover that 'we' are all feminists, liberals, advocates of gay liberation and the open curriculum; 'we' do not believe in God, or in any inherited religion; nor do the old ideas of authority, order and self-discipline carry weight for us. 'We' make up our minds as to the meaning of texts, by creating through our words the consensus that includes us. There is no constraint on us, beyond the community to which we have chosen to belong. And because there is no objective truth but only our own self-engendered consensus, our position is unassailable from any point of view outside it. The pragmatist can not only decide what to think; he can protect himself from whoever doesn't think the same.

A true pragmatist will no doubt invent history just as he invents everything else, by persuading 'us' to agree with him. Nevertheless, it is worth taking a glance at history, if only to see how paradoxical is Rorty's view of the human intellect. The Islamic *Ummah* – the society of all believers – was and remains the most extended consensus of opinion that the world has ever known. It expressly recognizes consensus (*ijma'*), as a criterion of, and indeed substitute for, truth, and is engaged in a never-ceasing endeavour to include as many as possible in its comprehensive first-person plural, while punishing apostasy as a crime. Moreover, whatever Rorty means by 'good' or 'better' beliefs, the pious Muslim must surely count as having some of the very best beliefs that bring security, stability, happiness, a handle on the world and a cheerful conscience as one blows up the *kafirs* who think otherwise. Yet still, is there not a nagging feeling somewhere that those heart-warming beliefs might not be true, and that the enervated opinions of the postmodern atheist might just have the edge on them? On Rorty's account of pragmatism, this is not something that a pragmatist can say, even though it is something that Rorty (who is not yet a Muslim) believes.

In its own eyes the Enlightenment involved the celebration of universal values and a common human nature. The art of the Enlightenment ranged over other places, other times and other cultures, in a heroic attempt to vindicate a vision of man as free and self-created. That vision inspired and was inspired by the old curriculum, and it has been the first concern of the postmodern university to put it in question. This explains the popularity of another relativist thinker – Edward Said, whose book *Orientalism* showed how to dismiss Enlightenment itself as a form of cultural imperialism.[58] The orient appears in Western art and literature, Said argues, as something exotic, unreal, theatrical and therefore unserious. Far from being a generous acknowledgement of other cultures, the orientalist art of Enlightenment Europe is an attempt to belittle them, and to reduce them to decorative episodes within the great imperium of Western progress.

Said's argument goes hand in hand with the advocacy of a 'multicultural' curriculum. The old curriculum, a product of the Enlightenment, is, he argues, monocultural, devoted to perpetuating the view of Western civilization as inherently superior to its rivals. It is also patriarchal, the product of Dead, White European Males, who have since lost their authority. And its assumption of a universal rational perspective, from the vantage-point of which all humanity could be studied, is nothing better than a rationalization of its imperialist ambitions. By contrast, we who live in the amorphous and multicultural environment of the postmodern city must open our hearts and minds to all cultures, and be wedded to none. The inescapable result of this is relativism: the recognition that no culture has any special claim to our attention, and that no culture can be judged or dismissed from outside.

But once again there is a paradox. For those who advocate this multicultural approach are, as a rule, vehement in their dismissal of Western culture. Said is no exception. While exhorting us to judge other cultures in their own terms, he is also asking us to judge Western culture from a point of view outside – to set it against alternatives and to judge it adversely, as ethnocentric and even racist.

---

58 *Orientalism*, New York: Pantheon Books, 1978.

Furthermore, the criticisms offered of Western culture are really confirmations of its claim to favour. It is thanks to the Enlightenment, and its universal view of human values, that racial and sexual equality have such a common-sense appeal to us. It is the universalist vision of man that makes us demand so much of Western art and literature – more than we should ever demand of the art and literature of Java, Borneo or China. It is the very attempt to embrace other cultures that makes Western art a hostage to Said's strictures – an attempt that has no parallel in the traditional art of Arabia, India or Africa. And it is only a very narrow view of our artistic tradition that does not discover in it a multicultural approach that is far more imaginative than anything that is now taught under that name. Our culture invokes an historical community of sentiment, while celebrating universal human values. It is rooted in the Christian experience, but draws from that source a wealth of human feeling that it spreads impartially over imagined worlds. From *Orlando Furioso* to Byron's *Don Juan*, from Monteverdi's *Poppeia* to Longfellow's *Hiawatha*, from *The Winter's Tale* to *Madama Butterfly*, our culture has continuously ventured into spiritual territory that has no place on the Christian map.

The Enlightenment, which set before us an ideal of objective truth, also cleared away the mist of religious doctrine. The moral conscience, cut off from religious observance, began to see itself from outside. At the same time, the belief in a universal human nature, so powerfully defended by Shaftesbury, Hutcheson and Hume, kept scepticism at bay. The suggestion that, in tracing the course of human sympathy, Shaftesbury and Hume were merely describing an aspect of 'Western' culture, would have been regarded by their contemporaries as absurd. The 'moral sciences', including the study of art and literature, were seen, in T. S. Eliot's words, as a 'common pursuit of true judgement'. And this common pursuit occupied the great thinkers of the Victorian age who, even when they made the first ventures into sociology and anthropology, believed in the objective validity of their results, and a universal truth that would emerge from them. And it did, as all readers of Frazer's *The Golden Bough* will acknowledge.

All that has changed utterly. In place of objectivity we have only 'inter-subjectivity' – in other words, consensus. Truths, meanings, facts and values are now regarded as negotiable. The curious thing, however, is that this woolly-minded subjectivism goes with a vigorous censorship. Those who put consensus in the place of truth, quickly find themselves distinguishing the true from the false consensus. Thus the consensus assumed by Rorty rigorously excludes all conservatives, traditionalists and reactionaries. Only liberals can belong to it; just as only feminists, radicals, gay activists and anti-authoritarians can take advantage of deconstruction; just as only the opponents of 'power' can make use of Foucault's techniques of moral sabotage; and just as only 'multiculturalists' can avail themselves of Said's critique of Enlightenment values. While holding that all cultures are equal and judgement between them absurd, the new relativism covertly appeals to the opposite belief. It is in the business of persuading us that Western culture and the traditional curriculum are racist, ethnocentric, patriarchal, and therefore beyond the pale of political acceptability. False though these accusations are, they presuppose the very universalist vision which they declare to be impossible.

The subliminal awareness of this paradox explains the popularity of thinkers like Foucault, Derrida and Rorty. Their arguments belong to a new species of theology: the theology of relativism. As in all theology, it is not the quality of the argument, but the nature of the conclusion, that renders the discussion acceptable. The relativist beliefs exist because they sustain a community – the new *ummah* of the disaffected. Hence the three thinkers that I have named share a duplicity of purpose: they seek on the one hand to undermine all claims to absolute truth, and on the other hand to uphold the orthodoxies upon which their congregation depends. The very reasoning which sets out to destroy the ideas of objective truth and absolute value imposes political correctness as absolutely binding, and cultural relativism as objectively true.

7

Religion and Enlightenment

Enlightenment, according to Kant, means 'the liberation of man from his self-imposed minority', the final assumption of a majority that is Reason's right and due.[59] Enlightenment is a tendency that is both inherent in Western civilization, and also constantly liable to be eclipsed by the human need for darkness. We are happier in Plato's cave than on the pinnacles above it, and the extreme form of Enlightenment – the scientism that chases all shadows away – is also a form of light pollution, which prevents us from seeing the stars. None the less, Enlightenment, of however mitigated a kind, is our recourse in every spiritual conflict, and in the encounter with Islam it has once again assumed its eighteenth-century character, as the distinguishing mark of our civilization.

Thinkers of the Enlightenment attacked religious doctrine, covertly assuming that religious behaviour is a result of religious belief, and will cease when the belief is refuted. And most religious beliefs are extremely easy to refute, or at any rate to put radically in question. Perhaps the sole exception to that generalization is the belief in the God of the philosophers, the 'love that moves the sun and the other stars', as Dante described Him, who enjoys the dubious benefit of hydra-like medieval arguments which spring two new heads for every one that has been logic-ed off. Even those arguments, however, began to look shaky in the

---

59 *What is Enlightenment?* in Hans Reiss (ed.), *Kant's Political Writings*, tr. H. B. Nisbet, Cambridge: CUP, 1970.

wake of Kant's *Critique of Pure Reason* and Hume's *Dialogues on Natural Religion*, and although Kant claimed to be defending faith against superstition, his writings – even *Religion within the Limits of Reason Alone* – leave the reader with the uncomfortable thought that maybe superstition is all that there is.

The Enlightenment View of Religion

The Enlightenment saw religion as founded in the belief in transcendental or supernatural beings, who are more powerful than we are, and who hold our destiny in their hands. In time, according to the Enlightenment view, people came to see the untenability of theological pluralism and settled down to believing in one God, whose wisdom, power and goodness set him so far above and beyond the world that he could be reached only by the *via negativa* of worship and prayer. Religion, as we know it, consists in that single belief, the doctrines that embellish it and the practices that stem from it – notably the moral trepidation that comes from the fear of God and the habit of turning up at his Sunday morning surgery.

That view of religion is doubtful for several reasons. For one thing, faith never has been and never will be the conclusion of an intellectual argument. Kant, who was acutely aware of the point, since he retained his faith after mounting the most withering refutation of its theological superstructure, argued that he attacked the claims of reason in order to make room for those of faith. It would be more honest to say that the claims of faith feature in his writings, as in the writings of all sincerely religious people, as premises, and never as conclusions. Rational enquiry may tell us what those premises mean. But it is only because they are lodged immovably in our worldview that the enquiry has a point for us.

The Genealogy of Faith

Once we see this we shall inevitably be tempted by the Nietzschean project of giving a 'genealogy' of religious belief. Whence does this belief arise, if it is not the result of intellectual speculation? How, and in response to what thoughts or experiences, does it change? And the simple and straightforward answer seems to be the right one. Religious belief is inherited from a community – typically the community into which you are born – and changes in response to changes in that community. Of course, it is also embellished by doctrine, and developed by rational enquiry. But the results of this enquiry become accepted into the religion only when the community has re-shaped itself so as to protect them from doubt. You can illustrate this from a study of the Reformation in Europe. But maybe it is easier to grasp the point by observing the Islamic sects in the Levant – in particular the Shi'ite, Druze, Ismaili and Alawite offshoots of the orthodox faith, whose doctrines are denounced by their neighbours as heresies precisely because they shape and are shaped by rival communities, conflicting loyalties and competing territorial claims. Intellectually speaking, what does it matter whether 'Ali was or was not the true successor of the Prophet? Emotionally speaking, it matters more than anything else, when this belief distinguishes my community, my loyalties and my territory from yours.

To put the point in another way: religion has its roots in the species-need to stand together, to claim and defend our territory and to make the kinds of sacrifice that are needed for our collective survival.[60] But we are rational animals, who furnish our biological needs with a justifying commentary. From the root of collective membership, therefore, grows the trunk of a common obedience and a collective inheritance of trust. And that trunk supports a branching superstructure of thought and emotion, which fills the hearts and the minds of believers, and changes their world. Religion embraces all those things – the root of membership, the trunk of obedience, the branches of faith and the leaf and flower of liturgy and worship. And to understand what it brings to us we must not examine only belief and doctrine, but also the way in which life with religion differs at every level from

---

60   Hence the field-day enjoyed by sociobiology in discussing the territory occupied by religion. See Scott Atran, *In Gods We Trust: The Evolutionary Landscape of Religion*, Oxford: OUP, 2002.

life without it. This is something that we should have learned from Durkheim's great classic, *Les formes élémentaires de la vie religieuse*. But it needs to be repeatedly reaffirmed, not least because the illusion persists among enlightened thinkers that religion consists merely in a set of beliefs, long ago disproved by science, but clung to nevertheless for the comfort that they afford.

Religion as a Social Fact

Piety and prayer are rooted in custom, and precede any formulation of their object. They are shaped by the needs of a community, and in turn give shape to it. That is why religious belief may be vague and obscure, but religious ceremony and pious conduct are always meticulous. Muhammad addressed this fact with a penetrating insight. He saw that his new religion must be attached to exact ceremonies, repeatable gestures, holy times and sacred places, if it was to win the hearts of his followers. The Koran is to be read as instructions for a pious life, not as a treatise of theology. Its theological claims can be summarized in three thoughts, namely, that there is only one God, that there is a day of judgement and that there is an afterlife in which the good will be rewarded and the wicked punished. Everything else is custom, ritual, law and example.

Durkheim was certainly not the first thinker to see religion as explained and understood in terms of our social needs and emotions. Comparative anthropology also grew out of the Enlightenment: it was a rational attempt to understand human difference, and to see both ancient customs and the newly discovered customs of Africa and America as manifestations of a universal human nature. Hence side by side with the Enlightenment view of religion as belief in the transcendental grew the study of religions as forms of social life, and the gradual recognition that belief in the transcendental is only one aspect of religion, and perhaps not the most significant. The thought gradually took shape among philologians and philosophers that the stories of the gods were not to be understood as attempts at literal truth, but as complex allegories of the human condition, whose real meaning was to be found in the workings of our deepest emotions. This thought culminated in the *Ring* of Wagner, in which religious ideas are returned, as it were, to their human origins, and in which the gods become dependent on the human dramas that they instigate and through which they seek a purely human redemption.

Wagner: Religion as Myth

Crucial to this view of religion is the idea that even when speaking directly of God or the gods, the religious consciousnesss is as it were translating from the literal to the metaphorical. Religion seems to be about the gods; in fact it is about us and our human destiny. But we can understand what it is saying only through analogy and allegory. The allegory transports us to another realm, where the dark secrets of the human soul can be spread out for our contemplation and made comprehensible in the guise of cosmic forces. That, for Wagner, is the essence of myth, and it is why myths are the core of ancient religion. For Wagner, as for the Greeks, a myth was not a decorative fairy-tale, but the elaboration of a secret, a way of both hiding and revealing mysteries that can be understood only in religious terms, through the ideas of sanctity, holiness and redemption. These are ideas that we all of us need, Wagner believed, and, although the common people perceive them through the veil of religious doctrine, they come alive in the great examples of love and renunciation, and find articulate form in art.[61] As Wagner put it: 'It is reserved to art to salvage the kernel of religion, inasmuch as the mythical images which religion would wish to be believed as true are apprehended in art for their symbolic value, and through ideal representation of those symbols art reveals the concealed deep truth within them'.[62]

---

61 See especially *Über Staat und Religion*, in *Gesammelte Schriften und Dichtungen* (second edn), Leipzig 1888, vol. viii, pp. 3–29.
62 *Die Religion und die Kunst*, in *Gesammelte Schriften und Dichtungen, op. cit.*, vol. x, p. 211.

Wagner took the view that religious doctrine had lost its power to convey the 'concealed deep truth' of our condition. Scientific scepticism and the social disorders of modernity threatened to bereave people of their religious beliefs. But people would still stand in need of their religious feelings, since these are deeply implanted in their social nature. Hence we need another route to those feelings, another way of being joined to the truth of our condition, so as to find the redemption that is promised by religion. This is the task that Wagner set himself in his art – to offer redemption without doctrine, and religious emotion without religious belief. It is the reason why he is both worshipped and hated as an artist.

Nietzsche: Religion as Cult

Nietzsche, profoundly influenced by Wagner, but with an acerbic anti-Christianity which – in my view – undermined his posture as an impartial anthropologist, also placed the kernel of religion elsewhere than in doctrine. For Nietzsche the fundamental phenomenon is the cult, something that Christianity shares with ancient religions. Through the cult people adopt the attributes of the god, and mysteriously identify with the god in his triumphs and ordeals. The doctrines associated with the cult are adopted because they are part of the fortifying experience, not because they are true. But they are believed to be true because they are fortifying – though true in a special way. Nothing can refute the doctrines, since they are neither arrived at nor relinquished through rational argument. They are holy mysteries, the proof of which lies in the cult itself. And the cult survives and grows because it fortifies the community of worshippers. In an important sense it tells them who they are, and with whom they belong.[63]

---

63   The thoughts that I attribute here to Nietzsche are not exactly his, but they are vividly suggested by *The Birth of Tragedy*, a source that ought to be more often acknowledged than it is.

Darwin: Religion as an Aid to Survival

Darwin himself had no theory of religion. But the rise of socio-biology and the discoveries of genetics have inevitably led to a large and growing literature devoted to the evolutionary explanation of the religious way of life. Some regard religions as 'memes' in the sense made familiar by Richard Dawkins: mental complexes that take up position in the brains of people, and use those brains, as a virus uses its host, to propagate themselves.[64] Others see religions as complex mental residues, derived from long-vanished contests in the struggle for survival. Others argue that religions exist and survive because they contribute to group selection,[65] creating the social cohesion and ability to sacrifice that give a competitive advantage to the communities that possess them.

The thesis that religions survive and spread because they are functional is by no means new, being defended from contrasting premises by Montesquieu, Hume, Feuerbach, Schopenhauer and Nietzsche. It is an inescapable observation, indeed, that religion has been universally applied to the task of securing marriage and the family against sexual predation – so ensuring the transference of social capital from one generation to the next. It is a small addition to argue that the capital in question is not just social but also genetic. However, this does nothing to explain the internal connections among religious beliefs or the connection between religious belief and religious practice. Why should the belief in the supernatural be associated everywhere with a concept of the sacred? Why should the concept of the sacred be rehearsed and implanted through meticulous rituals? And why should these

---

64   This is the position of Dawkins himself in *The Selfish Gene*, Oxford: OUP, 1989, and *Climbing Mount Improbable*, London: Viking Penguin, 1996. Dawkins takes a negative view of religion and describes it as a parasitic virus that destroys the life that it colonizes. Others, who accept the 'memetic' theory, are more open to the suggestion that religion is a symbiont or even a mutualist of the organisms in which it takes up residence – for example Daniel C. Dennett in *Breaking the Spell: Religion as a Natural Phenomenon*, London: Penguin, 2006.

65   For example David Sloan Wilson, *Darwin's Cathedral: Evolution, Religion and the Nature of Society*, Chicago: University of Chicago Press, 2002.

rituals be construed not as inexplicable mysteries, but as symbols of hidden truths – symbols, moreover, that we can learn to decipher, by re-creating them, as Wagner did, in works of art? I don't say that those questions are unanswerable; but for the time being they suggest that the sociobiological explanation of religion will not, in itself and without considerable refinement, help us to understand its meaning or to locate its real place in the human psyche.

The analogy with mathematics is useful. Mathematical competence is a decided evolutionary advantage, in protecting us from grievous and life-threatening errors. But it is advantageous because mathematics is true – objectively true. The sociobiology of mathematics won't give us access to its truth or in any way provide us with mathematical competence. Indeed, it will be strictly irrelevant to mathematical understanding and dependent upon the truth of mathematics for its own validation. The sociobiological theory of religion attempts to describe the evolutionary advantage to us of religion without reference to its truth – not because it assumes all religions to be false, but because it recognizes that their survival-inducing potential does not depend upon any particular set of metaphysical or magical doctrines. But maybe this survival-inducing potential depends nevertheless upon the 'concealed deep truth' that Wagner referred to. Until we explore the emotional, intellectual and symbolic structure of the religious form of life we will not know.

At this point the 'memeticist' will say that there are two entities whose survival is in question: the community of religious adherents and the religion that they share. The religion is a meme, which survives and flourishes by implanting itself in people. It may be, as Dawkins believes, a parasite that works to undermine its host; or it may be, as Dennett argues, merely a symbiont, which flourishes and declines without providing any necessary benefit to the life that harbours it.[66] In that case, however, we shall need to understand the nature of the religious meme. We shall need to explore what it is, how it enters the human

66   See *Breaking the Spell, op. cit.*

understanding, and what it provides to us by way of knowledge, sentiment and communal feeling. Like the mathematical meme, its survival might have something intimately to do with its truth. After all, the religions that survive seem to involve a powerful act of synthesis, whereby ritual, belief and symbolism are brought together in a manner not dissimilar to that involved in the creation of a work of art. This fact was apparent to Nietzsche, and to early anthropologists like Sir James Frazer, who attempted to give a typology of religious thought that would show just how the world is represented in the arcane but urgent symbols, gestures and stories of a living creed. And one suggestion that occurred to Frazer's disciples – notably to Jessie L. Weston, who was also a disciple of Wagner[67] – was that a religious way of thinking survives because it has engaged, at the deep level which only symbolism can reach, with lasting truths about the human condition. In short, the survival potential of religion is not, after all, so very different from that of mathematical competence, being a by-product of its truth-enshrining character. The difference is that the truths enshrined in a religion are not revealed in, but hidden by, its explicit doctrines, and made available to believers *through* their beliefs, but not *in* their beliefs.[68]

Girard: Religion as Sublimated Violence

In his celebrated book, *La violence et le sacré*, René Girard argues that the core of religion is not belief in the transcendental but the experience of sacred awe – an experience that is fundamental, he believes, to human community.[69] The sacred can be presented to us in many forms – in religious ritual, in prayer, in tragedy – but

---

67 See her classic account, *From Ritual to Romance*, London: David Nutt, 1912.
68 It would not follow from this that the religious meme is a mutualist *vis-à-vis* its host. All that is required is that its host is a truth-directed creature, one that sorts and selects from its mental contents according to the reality that is revealed in them.
69 *La violence et le sacré*, Paris: Grasset, 1972. See also *Le bouc émissaire*, Paris: Grasset, 1984.

its true origin is in an act of communal violence. Primitive societies, Girard argues, are invaded by 'mimetic desire', as rivals struggle to match each other's social and material acquisitions, so heightening antagonism and precipitating the cycle of revenge. The solution is to identify a victim, one marked by fate as 'outside' the community and therefore not entitled to vengeance against it, who can be the target of the accumulated blood-lust, and who can bring the chain of retribution to an end. Scapegoating is society's way of re-creating 'difference' and so restoring itself. By uniting against the scapegoat people are released from their rivalries and reconciled. Through his death the scapegoat purges society of its accumulated violence. His resulting sanctity is the long-term echo of the awe, relief and visceral re-attachment to the community that was experienced at his death.

The need for sacrificial scapegoating is, therefore, deeply implanted in the human psyche, arising from the very attempt to form a durable community in which the moral life can be successfully pursued. One purpose of the theatre is to provide fictional substitutes for the original crime, and so to obtain the benefit of moral renewal without the horrific cost. Hence, according to Girard, we should see a tragedy like Sophocles' *Oedipus Tyrannus* as a retelling of what was originally a ritual sacrifice, in which the victim is chosen so as to focus and confine the need for violence. The victim is thus both sacrificed and sacred, the source of the city's plagues and their cure. Girard rescues what he regards as the only valid part of Freud's notorious theory of the original parricide, as expounded in *Totem and Taboo*. Yes, Girard argues, collective murder is fundamental to religious communities: but not murder of a father; rather, murder of the victim, who may be himself accused of murdering the father, but whose death is required in order that the general need for aggression be satisfied. Through incest, kingship or worldly hubris the victim marks himself out as the outsider, the one who is not with us, and whom we can therefore sacrifice without renewing the cycle of revenge.

In time human sacrifice is replaced by the ritual sacrifice of animals – a process succinctly dramatized in the Old Testament story of Abraham and Isaac. And the omnipresence of animal offerings in Mediterranean religion – from the offerings made by Cain and Abel, to those made by every Muslim at the feast of 'Eid – is taken by Girard as a deep confirmation of his insight into the connection between ceremonial death and the experience of the sacred.[70]

Taking Stock

I don't doubt that there is something drastic about Girard's theory and that it owes much of its appeal to its own kind of intellectual violence. But I am also drawn to it, as I am drawn to both Nietzsche's and Wagner's – not as full explanations of the nature of the religious experience, but as imaginative explorations of the dark origins of religion in the first human communities. These theories seem to summarize in a striking way facts with which we are familiar, and which are otherwise wholly strange to us. All three thinkers were fascinated by the supreme sacrifice of Christ, who offered to prove his divine origin and mission by voluntarily surrendering himself for the sacrifice that society required. And all three look behind the naïve Enlightenment view of religion, as a species of intellectual delusion, to present the striking counter-assertion, that religion is a species of emotional truth, but a truth that is not aware of itself, and could not become aware of itself without ceasing to be.

Wagner and Nietzsche were not the first to take this external view of religion, as a psychic phenomenon whose truth is misrepresented by the intellectual doctrines which protect it from

---

70   This is not the place to review all the objections that have been made to Girard. But see Walter Burkert, *Homo Necans: The Anthropology of Ancient Greek Sacrificial Ritual and Myth*, tr. Peter Bing, Berkeley, CA: University of California Press, 1983; J.-P. Vernant's rebuttal of Burkert, 'Théorie générale du sacrifice et mise à mort dans la *Thusia* grecque', in *Le sacrifice dans l'antiquité*, Entretiens Hardt 27, Geneva 1981; J. Z. Smith, 'The Domestication of Sacrifice', in R. G. Hamerton-Kelly (ed.), *Violent Origins*, Stanford: Stanford University Press, 1987, pp. 191–205; Paul Veyne, 'Inviter les dieux, sacrifier, banqueter: quelques nuances de la religiosité gréco-romaine', *Annales HSS*, 2000, no. 1, pp. 3–42, and Robert Parker, 'Sacrifice and Battle', in Hans van Wees (ed.), *War and Violence in Ancient Greece*, London: Duckworth, 2000, pp. 299–314.

argument. Feuerbach and David Strauss (the first a commanding influence on Wagner) had already laid the groundwork.[71] But it was Wagner and Nietzsche who set the agenda for the anthropological study of religion, the first through his attempt to retrieve the religious experience through art, the second through his desire to live without the religious experience altogether.[72] Nietzsche's celebrated remark, made shortly before his madness, that 'we have art less we perish of the truth', shows how little he succeeded, and how close he was, at the end as at the beginning, to Wagner. Nevertheless, his enormous influence in recent times is due to his attempts to cast off the religious yoke, to become a 'free spirit' who does not merely reject religious doctrine, but who lives in a world in which religion has been *overcome*. As he recognized, in his theory of the *Übermensch*, the overcoming of religion would require the overcoming of man, and a life 'beyond good and evil', a life of utter and unbearable loneliness. Nietzsche went mad before getting to that point. His example ought to be a warning to us.

The Wagnerian, Nietzschean, Girardian and Darwinian approaches to religion are not incompatible, nor can any of them claim to be the whole truth about a phenomenon which has been the greatest motor in human history. Observing the Shi'ite remembrance of Karbala, in which the death of Husain is re-enacted in a collective self-flagellation, you might well be tempted to say – 'so *this* is what true religion is', and then you will side with Nietzsche and Girard. Observing a Quaker meeting of Friends, or reading a sermon by John Donne or Lancelot Andrewes, you might be tempted to say the same, and in that case

---

71 The study of ancient myth and religion as giving form to universal psychic realities was, however, already common in German culture before the young Hegelians made a fetish of it, not least because of Hegel himself. The true origin of the approach was probably Georg F. Creuzer's *Symbolik und Mythologie der alten Völker*, Leipzig: Darmstadt, 1810–12, a work that caused much controversy in its day.

72 To my knowledge only Claude Lévi-Strauss, in the prelude to *The Raw and the Cooked*, Paris: Plon, 1964, trs. J. and D. Weightman, London, 1978, and Jessie L. Weston in *From Ritual to Romance*, *op. cit*, give Wagner the credit that all anthropologists owe to him.

you will see religion as the Enlightenment saw it, as a belief in and posture towards the transcendental. And yet you will also know, without being able to explain, that the self-flagellating Shi'ite and the serene Anglican preacher are at some level engaged in exactly the same practice, and that the meaning of this practice lies in the community that it shapes.

A Synthetic Account

The simplest response to those observations is, therefore, to say that religion is both a ritual reaffirmation of membership, and a stance towards the transcendental. After all, we are rational beings. We do not experience our social membership as horses experience their membership of the herd. We think about it, explain it, try to understand and justify. Faced with inherited rituals, we ask ourselves whence they came and to what they lead. Death is a monstrous fact for us, as it is not for other animals; time and eternity are present in all our thoughts, and the simplest explanation of our sacrificial rituals is that we do them because they are commanded, and that the power that commands them will also reward our obedience. Even if Girard is right in thinking that the sense of the sacred has its origins in the mimetic violence of the tribe, the rational soul moves inevitably towards the belief in transcendental beings. This belief, which begins in wonder and ends in faith, conscripts the sacred to its purpose, as proof of a world beyond. It is not just because we are social beings, with emotions rooted in a past of solemn sacrifice and ritual cults, that we distinguish sacred from profane, and sanctity from desecration. We instinctively connect the sacred with the transcendental, seeing holy places, times and rituals as windows on to another realm – places in the empirical world where we look out in astonishment at something that we can understand through ritual and prayer, which we try to explain through theological doctrine, but which always in the end eludes our attempt to describe it.

However we look at it, the legacy of comparative anthropology forbids us from taking the simple Enlightenment view of religion, as a form of intellectual error. Religion is a stance towards the world, rooted in social membership, and influencing every aspect of experience, emotion and thought. In trying to understand our own situation, in a world where religion is under assault from a relentless tide of secularization, we should move away from questions of doctrine and address instead the whole state of mind of religious people, as blasphemy and sacrilege invade their sacred spaces and as they strive nevertheless to retain their innocence, their obedience and their faith.

Religious people see the world in a way that enlightened people may not see it. Not only do they possess faith, belief in the transcendental and hopes and fears regarding providence and the afterlife. Their world is parcelled out by concepts of the holy, the forbidden, the sacred, the profane and the sacramental. These concepts may be absent from the intellectual life of faithless people. But, if the counter-enlightenment view of religion has any truth in it, they are rooted in feelings that even faithless people have. Hence secularization does not impact only on the thoughts and feelings of religious people. It impacts on the thoughts and feelings of everyone, causing radical changes in the experience of social membership, in the structure of the *Lebenswelt*, as Husserl called it (i.e. the world as lived), and in the way human conduct is perceived and described.

Secularization: The First Wave

To see that this is so we should distinguish two waves of secularization. The first, characterized by nineteenth-century Europe, involves a wavering of religious faith, and a retreat of religious ideas, beliefs and symbols from the public sphere. As people lost the metaphysical beliefs to which their habits of piety and worship had been pinned, they tried to shore up their social world in other ways – through secular law and institution-building. The sacrament of marriage was recast as a civil agreement; old customs of courtship and child-bearing were justified in new ways, by reference to the needs of society and patriotic duty. The churches withdrew or were expelled from the political process and from the institutions of civil society, and these in turn were provided with secular dignities to shore up their old authority. The outward form of society remained more or less unaltered as faith withdrew. And people experienced their social membership not as a form of submission to God but as a kind of individual commitment, made sacred by a purely human love. This is what Matthew Arnold conveys in his famous lines from 'Dover Beach':

> The Sea of Faith
> Was once, too, at the full, and round earth's shore
> Lay like the folds of a bright girdle furled.
> But now I only hear
> Its melancholy, long, withdrawing roar,
> Retreating, to the breath
> Of the night-wind, down the vast edges drear
> And naked shingles of the world.

Having expressed thus the retreat of faith from the public sphere, Arnold begins the next stanza with a passionate invocation of the private sphere:

> Ah, love, let us be true
> To one another!

In other words, let us replace God's love with our human love, so that the world remains meaningful to us, in something like the way it was meaningful before, when God was in his heaven and the nymphs and dryads in their groves. (The same idea, exalted into a comprehensive vision of human destiny, animates Wagner's *Ring*, in which the gods themselves discover that only human love contains the seeds of redemption, and that human love is a relation between dying things.)

Arnold typifies the Victorian attempt to patch up the social world after the retreat of faith, using purely human resources. Individuals can lose their faith within the context of a religious community, and still inhabit the common *Lebenswelt*, seeing the world as marked out by the customs, institutions and perceptions that are the legacy of religion. This is what we witness in the writings of nineteenth-century secularists, such as John Stuart Mill, Jules Michelet or Henry Thoreau. Their world bears the stamp of a shared religion; the human form for them is still divine; the free individual still shines in their world with a more than earthly illumination, and the hidden goal of all their writings is to enoble the human condition. Such writers did not experience their loss of faith as a loss, since in a very real sense they hadn't lost religion. They had rejected various metaphysical ideas and doctrines, but still inhabited the world that faith had made – the world of secure commitments, of marriage and love, of obsequies and christenings, of real presences in ordinary lives and exalted visions in art. Their world, like Matthew Arnold's and Wagner's, was a world where the sacred, the forbidden and the sacramental were widely recognized and socially endorsed.

This condition found idealized expression in the Gothic revival, and in the writings of its principal high Victorian advocate, John Ruskin. Nobody knows whether Ruskin was a vestigial Christian believer, a fellow-traveller or an atheist profoundly attached to the medieval vision of a society ordered by faith. His exhortations, however, are phrased in the diction of the Book of Common Prayer; his response to the science and art of his day is penetrated by the spirit of religious inquisition, and his recommendations to the architect are for the building of the Heavenly Jerusalem, the vision of which had been granted to him in St Mark's. The Gothic style, as he described and commended it, was to recapture the sacred for a secular age. It was to offer visions of sacrifice and consecrated labour, and so counter the dispiriting products of the industrial machine. It would be, in the midst of our utilitarian madness, a window on to the transcendental, where once again we could pause and wonder, and where our souls would be filled with the light of forgotten worlds. The Gothic revival – both for Ruskin and for the atheist William Morris – was an attempt to re-consecrate the city, as an earthly community united in a shared acknowledgement of sacred things.

The attack on the Gothic revival by the modernists – by the Bauhaus, Le Corbusier, Pevsner and others – was part of the second wave of secularization. The attack began with a call to honesty. The message was: 'We no longer believe, so why pretend?' Why pretend that the city is a holy place, rather than a place that serves merely human purposes? Why deck out our buildings with symbols of the transcendental, when we have ceased entirely to believe in it? This, surely, was the real motive behind architectural modernism, and it is what explains the puritanical and iconoclastic fervour of that movement. Modernism was sweeping away the old religion, in the name of a new social order that was to dispense with the gods. (Hence the modernist hostility to mouldings, which create the shadows in which the last shy gods can hide.)

Secularization: The Second Wave

Modernism in architecture went hand in hand with socialist and fascist projects to rid old Europe of its hierarchical past, to re-shape it as a godless but orderly society, which would live in honest recognition that it is man, not God, who is the final purpose. Secularization was no longer content with shoring up the old institutions from purely human resources. The old institutions had to be destroyed and replaced with purely man-made and functional devices that would meet the needs of a society that had cast off the fetters of religious dogma. This second wave of secularization launched itself with a plethora of manifestoes – modernist, futurist, dadaist, symbolist, communist – by way of announcing the absolute break with the past that the puritanical atheists of the nineteenth century had been so reluctant to make. It began, in short, with a self-conscious attempt to believe in itself. But the attempt didn't last. Once the Second World War (itself a product of modernist ideas) was over, the second wave of secularization proceeded apace, not as a form of belief, but as a systematic revision in the way the human world is perceived. The human being is now situated among his technological discoveries, unshackled, empowered, but without a destination. For many this has induced a vagueness and cynicism about the nature and destiny of humanity, together with an ever-expanding permissiveness that has wiped away the last depositories of the sacred from their world.

This second wave of secularization has changed entirely the experience of ordinary people in modern societies. Whatever the state of their faith, and whatever community they may identify in their hearts as theirs, they find themselves in the midst of a culture of widespread desecration, in which human relations are voided of the old religious virtues – innocence, sacrifice and eternal vows – and in which little or no public acknowledgement is afforded to ideas of the sacred, the holy and the forbidden. Our institutions and our cities are alike entirely secular, with no inner sanctuary where the old gods can hide. Our art is full of sacrilegious images and satires of the godly. And the city is being blown apart by a new kind of joke architecture, which has put aside the puritanical discipline of the modernists in order to remind us that there is no permanence, no eternity, no heavenly city to be built in stone, but only a facetious, glassy laughter.

The Transformation of the *Lebenswelt*

In short, religion has disappeared from our social context. Even if we individually adhere to a faith of our own, it can only be in the consciousness that the world itself rejects it. In so far as there is a shared *Lebenswelt* it is not that of our ancestors, shaped by the concepts and experiences of religious faith, but an entirely novel product, from which the idea of human distinction, of the sacred nature of our form and the consecration of our loves has been driven away. Hence we do not experience the human body as something removed from nature and destined for a higher sphere. Its appearance has changed from that of a divinity to that of an animal, rooted in the natural world and obedient to its dark imperatives. This is not just a change in our beliefs: it is a change in our perceptions. The loss of religion manifests itself *phenomenologically*.

This is strikingly confirmed by a visit to any art gallery. The human figure has been banished from much modern painting: if it appears at all it is in the form of a photographic image, in other words, an image generated mechanically, which presents the raw, physical fact. In Corot, Monet, Cézanne, Renoir; in Winslow Homer and Edward Hopper, figures in a landscape stand out as visitations, centres of selfhood and judgement, which fill their surroundings with images of freedom. Now figures in a landscape are usually no more than that – figures, animals with clothes on, coloured shapes with a human outline.

It is very hard for us to live with the new perception of the human body. Everything in us points back to that religious vision from which we have strayed, telling us that the human form is sacred, untouchable and an object of awe. Hence we experience a profound conflict in our feelings, and a virulent desire to desecrate, to drag the human body down to its animal essentials and to show it as pure object, in which the light of selfhood and freedom has been extinguished. Sartre gives a beautiful description of this process in his account of sado-masochism.[73] But things have moved on since *Being and Nothingness*. We live now in a world in which erotic feelings can no longer be easily rescued from the desecrating maelstrom of pornography, in which the human body is reduced to panting chunks on the screen, in which children are brought up on images that show the body not as the place where empirical and transcendental meet, the I-hole in the screen of nature, but as a target, a thing to be assaulted, ravaged and consumed, to be shown in all its contortions as a squirming, needing, agonizing worm.

Those sexual and sadistic images both shape and are shaped by our new perception of death, as something alien, unmentionable or even laughable in the manner of other bodily functions. My death is no longer a part of life, the great transition for which all else is preparation. It comes to me from outside, when the great machine suddenly turns in my direction, and I too am swallowed. Hand in hand with the ceaseless morbid portrayal of death on the screen, therefore, goes a flight from death and from the thought of death in everyday life. The cherishing of each other, which is the

---

73 See *Being and Nothingness*, tr. Hazel E. Barnes, New York: Philosophical Library, 1956, Book III, ch. 3.

lived experience of our mortality, withers away, as does the habit of paying tribute to the dead, and being at one with them in our thoughts. A society in flight from death is also in flight from life. Refusing to believe that the worst will happen, we cannot see that the best requires it – that whatever makes life worthwhile, be it love, adventure, children, settling, has death as its price. We lose the 'tragic sense of life', as Unamuno called it, and with it the capacity to live life to the full.

The Problematization of the Animals

To the extent that we see people as animals, the animals themselves become problematic to us. Having fallen to the sphere that is theirs, we look on them as we look on people. Hence arises that strange movement, into which has been poured an enthusiasm that itself has much of the religious about it, for 'animal liberation' and 'animal rights'. It is possible to prove by dense philosophical argument that the other animals are metaphysically distinct from us, and that, properly interpreted, the old view that we, but not they, have souls, is true – though the word 'soul' would form no part of the proof.[74] It is possible to show that there are no grounds for attributing rights to animals or for believing that they either desire or are capable of 'liberation'. Nevertheless, philosophical argument is of no help in dissuading people who don't understand the point, since philosophical arguments, unlike religious beliefs, do not issue in perceptions. In the *Lebenswelt* as religion shapes it, an animal occupies a different place from a person. An animal is not seen as a centre of selfhood and freedom. It is not a source of shame or judgement, but a normal part of the empirical world, sharing some of our feelings with us, but never aspiring to the noble, the true or the good. From that perception of animals stems the old morality, that forbade us to treat people as animals or animals as people. But when the perception dwindles and disappears, so, too, does the traditional morality.

---

74   See my *Animal Rights and Wrongs* (third edn), London: Metro Books, 2001.

Again, we might look to art as an illustration of what I mean. In Titian's nudes you will find, beside the body of the woman, a lap-dog, serenely observing this expanse of flesh. Dogs have no conception of what it is to be naked, and their calm unembarrass-ability before the sight of human flesh reminds us of how very different the human form is, in their eyes and in ours. In this way Titian returns us to the Garden of Eden, instructing us that we are not to see this body as naked, as though the woman were exposing herself to us, in the manner of the girl on Page Three. The nude's sexuality is not offered to *us*, but remains latent and expectant within her – awaiting the lover to whom it can be offered not shamelessly, but nevertheless without shame. The dog reminds us that she, unlike him, is capable of shame, while being neither ashamed nor shameless. In other words, she is a moral being, bearer of the religiously engendered virtues of innocence and shame. This stupendous fact is presented to us not as a thought or a theory, but as a revelation – the kind of revelation that, for the religious view of things, is contained in every human form, but which is of necessity hidden by our daily commerce and retrieved and clarified by art. Titian's nude is exactly what the Bible says she is, a creature made in God's image, as different from the dog that is watching her as God is different from the world.

In such a work of art we encounter the difference between human and animal as a phenomenological fact – and one with momentous consequences. For many people today, however, it is not a fact at all, but an illusion. As I say, I think that they are wrong: but the argument that would show them to be wrong is one that they will resist to the end, for the reason that their experience can make no sense of it.

Repudiating the Sacred

The second wave of secularization, I have suggested, involves an attempt to rid the world of the sacred, the forbidden and the sacramental. This attempt is not consciously made, any more than children consciously try to free themselves from the home or jealous lovers consciously enumerate the failings of their rivals. Like religion itself, secularization is a social process, propelled by an invisible hand towards a goal that nobody need intend and everybody may regret. Moreover, the second wave of secularization has about it a kind of urgency, an intemperate dislike of opposition and a refusal to countenance dissent that are reminiscent of religious sects. You see this, for example, in the American movements in favour of abortion and gay marriage. Both of those practices threaten ancient feelings about the sacred and the sacramental, but both are regarded by many of their advocates as causes from which it is deepest heresy to dissent. Likewise the movement to remove prayers from public schools, to forbid courthouses to display the Ten Commandments, to remove all reference to God from the coinage and public symbols of the United States – these are not, as a rule, mildly voiced opinions, issued by people who wonder just how far they should impose their views on their believing fellow-citizens. They are passionate causes, often pursued with a zealotry that only religions are normally thought to promulgate.

In short, the second wave of secularization, after a period of cynicism and doubt, has given rise to a curious simulacrum of the religious frame of mind. The new distaste for heresy and desire for conformity suggest that secular ideology is now attempting to fill the gap left by the old form of social membership. But this ideology is unlike the religious frame of mind in a crucial particular, namely that it has no clear conception of the sacred, the consecrated or the sacramental. Its rituals are spare and uncertain and its occasions for awe non-existent – or almost so.

The Enduring Need

But this is where the picture becomes difficult to decipher. If you look at Western societies from the angle of traditional religion you will see a seemingly inexorable flood of desecration, directed not at religious symbols, but at the thing on which they all depend – the human body and the human face. But if you look at our societies with the eyes of an anthropologist, seeking to understand the well-springs of our social emotions, you will uncover quite a different picture. You will discover outbreaks of millenarian religion (Jonestown, Waco, etc.); you will observe religious movements like The Nation of Islam, founded in far-fetched myths but promising redemption in the midst of squalor. You will be struck by the celebrity cults, which mirror the cults of local saints and local gods. You will discover gods that have died and been resurrected like Elvis. You will uncover acts of ritual sacrifice, in which the celebrity is murdered like John Lennon, as the supreme tribute of a love that could not bear him to remain longer on this polluted earth.

You will even find the ritual scapegoating described by René Girard, as in the strange canonization of Princess Diana, when those who had, in their pitiless prurience, hounded the princess to her death, wandered in bewildered crowds, vaguely hoping for her reincarnation and begging absolution from her ghost. We witnessed then the primordial yearning for the sacred as Girard describes it, a yearning reaching back to the very earliest dream-pictures of mankind.

And you will find too a kind of Satanic attempt to catch last glimpses of the sacred, in the actions that wipe it away. It is this, I believe, that explains the extraordinary rise in child pornography – a practice that is not confined to the images that are available on the Internet, but to the most ordinary ways that people have adopted of dressing and addressing their children. The 8-year-old girl in G-string and ear-rings is simultaneously childlike and knowing, a creature torn between worlds, and on the verge of desecration. By dressing their children in this way, and encouraging them to copy the lubricious dances and sensual throes of their parents, people are conjuring out of the sewer of desecration a last, sad image of the human form in its innocence, as the currents of pollution bear it away.

To cut a long story short, I do not believe that the second wave of secularization, for all its quasi-religious zeal, has reduced the religious needs of our species. We may have lost belief in the transcendental. But our hunger for the sacred still seems to erupt into the public world, in grotesque forms that would be comic were they not signs of a deep emotional disorder – of a refusal to accept the sacred in the only form that has actually been offered to us.

A Note on 9/11

Those thoughts are relevant, I believe, to the September 11 massacre. This was carried out by people whose sense of the sacred had been deeply offended by modernity – not merely by modern manners and the tide of desecration which the second wave of secularization had spread across the world, but by the destruction of the old Muslim city, and by the erection in its stead of the insolent towers for which Le Corbusier set the precedent in Algiers. Mohammed Atta went to Germany to study architecture, not to absorb the sacrilegious postmodernism that is the only accepted language there, but to write a thesis on the old Muslim city of Aleppo, and to explore how it might be restored to its former character, following the destruction wrought by Hafiz al-Assad in his exterminatory war against the Muslim brotherhood. The old Muslim city is a sacred place, in which no building can rise higher than the mosque, where streets are gulleys between aedicules and mouldings, and where all doors give on to places that are cool, quiet and sacrosanct. The assault on America was an assault on the American city, and on the American *concept* of the city, as a place opened up, surrendered to human functions and removed from divine jurisdiction – the city of Lewis Mumford, though not, I think, that of Jane Jacobs. Again, if you looked on this event with the eye of a René Girard, you would discover, at the heart of it, an act of ritual sacrifice, in which death is summoned to re-sacralize the modern city, and to punish its secular ways. And you will understand, then, why this terrible crime was greeted by so many Muslims with spasms of collective jubilation. Neither those who committed the crime nor those who rejoiced in it were conscious of the real source of their emotion: but then, that is exactly what the comparative study of religion tells us, namely, that religious feelings are rooted below the level of consciousness, and have a natural tendency to be misunderstood by those who are in their grip – a tendency that contributes, indeed, to their survival.

Our Situation

Here, then, is how I would describe our current situation, at the end of the second wave of secularization. It is a situation without precedent, so far as I can see, in the history of the world, and one which people may endorse in their heads but are in many cases unable to accept in their hearts. Western societies are organized by secular institutions, secular customs and secular laws, and there is little or no mention of the transcendental either as the ground of worldly authority or the ultimate court of appeal in all our conflicts. This situation is not new: it was with us in the nineteenth century, when it co-existed with widespread religious faith among the people, and a respectful scepticism among the elite. New, however, is the widespread repudiation of the sacred – the chasing away of divine shadows from the life of the city, the life of the body, the life of the emotions and the life of the mind. Attempts at sacramental relations like marriage are scorned, and marriage itself reconstituted as a contract, in the way I described earlier, in Chapter 6. Custom and ceremony have no real place in modern life. With the evaporation of the sacred comes the vanishing of the religious virtues of innocence, piety and shame.

When we look back at Victorian society, we are tempted to admire the achievements of that first wave of secularization. Religious tolerance, private security and individual freedom had all been achieved, by the simple expedient of government based in secular laws. At the same time the religious virtues had remained in place – manifest nowhere more evidently than in the lives of the righteous atheists who were taking charge of things. (Think of Mill's *Autobiography*, for example: what a picture of innocence is there!) The city had not yet been sacrificed to its function, nor had custom and ceremony ceased to exert their benign jurisdiction over the lives of ordinary people.

We have retained some of those good things: notably the religious tolerance and private security that secular law make possible. In many respects we also enjoy as much, if not more freedom than our Victorian forebears. But the freedoms we enjoy are freedoms that they would not have countenanced, indeed, which they would have seen as profoundly destructive of the social order. The Victorians had managed to retain the image of the sacred in place, as one might retain a fresco while rebuilding the wall to which it clings. (That, in my view, is a truer description of Ruskin and the Gothic revival than the banal charge of dishonesty.) But the second wave of secularization has wiped this image from the public face of Western society.

The first wave of secularization offered no real offence to the religious way of life. Communities could enjoy, under its tolerant protection, the deeper and more heartfelt protection of their gods, who encountered no sacrilege to provoke them. The second wave of secularization is more difficult for religious communities to bear. Nor do the vacillating, doubt-based communities of modern cities seem better able to cope with it. The hunger for the sacred and the repudiation of the sacred contend unceasingly in the hearts of our citizens today, and if, from time to time, this contest erupts in violence, we should not be surprised. Nor should we be surprised that there are people who hope for the final destruction of our societies, as a punishment for their blatant sacrilege.

Living with Sacrilege

Modern writers and artists have devoted much energy to recuperating the experience of the sacred – but as a private, rather than a public, form of consciousness. Poets like Rilke and Eliot; artists such as Edward Hopper and Stanley Spencer; composers like Schoenberg and Stravinsky – all present us with an inner life made holy by dedication, and with the human form re-made in the image of God. Such was the great mission of modernist art, during the early years of the twentieth century, a mission betrayed by the architects but adhered to almost universally by composers, painters and poets. But modernist art was directed at the few, and has never appealed to the many; it has now been superseded by pop for the many and postmodernism for the few. And pop and postmodernism offer no barriers to desecration.

So how do modern societies cope with the second wave of secularization? What practice or institution can help them to live with a de-sacralized world? It is well for Nietzsche to say that we have art so that we shall not perish from the truth. But most people don't have art: kitsch, pop and porn have driven art to the margins of their lives. And although kitsch, pop and porn don't tell the truth, their lies are de-meaning lies: lies which eliminate *meaning.*

It is partly a result of the Enlightenment view of religion that we believe that we can solve the problems caused by secularization simply by granting religious freedom. If religion is primarily a matter of belief and doctrine, then by allowing freedom of belief, and freedom to discuss and proselytize, it is thought, we ensure that people will make their own religious space, communities will be able to worship God in their own way, and rival faiths will live side by side in mutual toleration. However, the Enlightenment view is profoundly wrong. Belief and doctrine are a part of religion, certainly; but so too are custom, ceremony, ritual, membership, sacrifice, the division between sacred and profane and the visceral hostility to sacrilege. By allowing religious freedom we do nothing to create a public world in which religious communities can feel truly at home. Moreover, it is naïve to think that every kind of religious community can be governed by a secular jurisdiction. The idea of such a jurisdiction is a construct of Roman law, inherited by Christianity, and crystallized by the Enlightenment. Secular jurisdiction has no authority in Islamic thinking, and Western societies earn no favours in Muslim eyes by extending to Muslims the protection of a godless rule of law.

I have no final answer to the dilemmas that I have just exposed. But let me conclude with a positive suggestion. We cannot turn back the second wave of secularization, any more than Matthew Arnold could have summoned back the tide of faith. But we can strive to be gentle with its victims – to recognize that ordinary people, when they ask that prayers be said in their children's schools, that offensive images be removed from TV screens and hoardings, that the outward signs of the religious life be publicly endorsed, are giving voice to feelings which we may think we have grown out of, but which, in fact, at the unconscious level where they thrive, we still experience.

Anthropologists quickly learn compassion and sympathy towards the tribes they study. We should follow their example when looking on the tribe that is ours. Most of all, we should learn that religion, properly understood, is an immovable part of the human condition, manifest as much in the 'free spirits' who sneer at it as in the pious souls for whom it is the fount of consolation. It is surely time for the law to distance itself from sacrilege, and to recognize that our hard-won political freedoms ought not to include the freedom to poison the most precious emotions that we have.

8

The Totalitarian Temptation

Totalitarian government is government by a centralized power structure, which is neither limited by law nor self-limited by a constitution, and which extends into every aspect of social life.[75] Totalitarian ideology is the system of ideas and doctrines that justify and normalize the totalitarian form of government, usually by representing it as the reign of justice, maybe even as the 'final solution' to a social problem that can be solved in no other way.

Clearly, on that definition, totalitarian government is a matter of degree. A government may be to some extent constrained by law, even if able to overrule the law in special cases; it may present itself behind the mask of a constitution, even if the constitution is of only limited effectiveness in reducing its power. The important point is not the extent of the totalitarian lawlessness, but the absence of any fundamental constraint on the central authority, and the assumption that every aspect of society, however remote from the normal concerns of government, is one

---

75 There is an extensive literature concerning the distinction between totalitarian and authoritarian government and the observable marks of totalitarian power. See C. J. Friedrich (ed.), *Totalitarianism*, Cambridge, MA: Harvard University Press, 1954; L. Schapiro, *Totalitarianism*, London: Macmillan, 1983 (on the fascist's use and endorsement of the term); Hannah Arendt, *The Origins of Totalitarianism*, Harmondsworth: Penguin, 1982 (for eighteenth-century antecedents) and R. Scruton, 'Totalitarianism and the Rule of Law', in Ellen Frankel Paul (ed.), *Totalitarianism at the Crossroads*, New Brunswick, NJ and London: Transaction Books, 1990. See also the classic and controversial study of the Soviet example by J. L. Talmon, *The Origins of Totalitarian Democracy*, London: Mercury Books, 1964.

over which the central government can, should it choose, exert control.

Those influenced by Hegel might express the point in another way, by saying that a totalitarian government is one that does not respect or acknowledge the distinction between civil society and State. The State is the final authority in all matters of social choice, and nothing limits the power of the State in the way that it might be limited by a representative legislature or a system of judge-made, or judge-discovered, law. Under totalitarian rule society is itself a creation of the State, rather than the other way round, and those who can claim the protection of the State have an insuperable advantage over their neighbours in the competition for scarce resources.

In East Central Europe totalitarian goverment was imposed by political parties, following the principle of 'democratic centralism' invented by Lenin and later copied by Hitler. The party was a quasi-military organization, quite unlike anything that would be called a political party in the Western world today. It did not try to extend its membership but, on the contrary, tried to restrict its membership to those who could be relied upon to carry out the centrally issued commands. Joining the party was a privilege, not a right. Members were rewarded for their obedience with social benefits that could not conceivably be enjoyed by ordinary citizens. In this way the Communist Party generated, as Djilas expressed it, a 'new class', known in Russian as the *nomenklatura*, whose privileges were far more secure than those enjoyed by previous aristocracies, since they did not arise 'by an invisible hand' from social interaction but were imposed from above by the State. Society was controlled by the State, the State was controlled by the party, and the party was controlled from the top by the leadership. Because it was conceived in military terms, the party could not depend upon the existing civil law to exert its discipline, but had to bend the law to its purposes. Henceforth, the law ceased to be a means of settling social disputes and establishing justice and became a device for punishing those who deviated from the party line.

We should not deceive ourselves into thinking that totalitarianism is simply a twentieth-century phenomenon, or one invented by Lenin. The desire to organize society on military principles, and to exert a top-down control over every social initiative, the economy included, has antecedents in the slave societies of the ancient Middle East. It has been widely observed in the Far East and Africa, and has erupted into European politics many times prior to the twentieth century. The recent experience of totalitarianism in Europe was foreshadowed at the French Revolution, when the Committee of Public Safety acted in the same way as the Nazi and Communist Parties, setting up 'parallel structures' through which to control the State and to exert a micromanagerial tyranny over every aspect of social life. Recent scholarship, which has tended to look on the French Revolution without the rosy spectacles worn by the nineteenth-century advocates of liberty and the rights of man, has also tended to the conclusion that its significance is to be found more in the Terror than in the liberal slogans that disguised it.[76]

Let us at least be realistic, and recognize that, if totalitarian governments have arisen and spread with such rapidity in modern times, this is because there is something in human nature to which they correspond and on which they draw for their moral energy. It is characteristic of intellectuals to believe that the totalitarian temptation is a temptation in the realm of ideas: a temptation to error, of a kind that can be witnessed in the false theories of the early socialists. The intellectual critics of communism trace the tyranny of the system to the refuted labour theory of value, to the inversion of cause and effect in the theory of base and superstructure, to the simplistic idea of class struggle, and to the potential contradiction in the idea that classes are both the by-products and the agents of social change. On this view Terror is just error with a capital T.

Now there is no doubt that totalitarian ideology is replete with intellectual confusions, and that Marxism is responsible for many of them. But not everything in Marx is false, and one of his

---

76   See François Furet, *Penser la Révolution Française*, Paris: Gallimard, 1978, 1983; René Sedillot, *Le coût de la Révolution Française*, Paris: Perrin, 1987; Simon Schama, *Citizens*, London: Penguin, 1999.

theories is particularly relevant to the understanding of totalitarianism, which is the theory of ideology itself. Marx understood 'ideology' as a set of ideas, doctrines and myths that exist because of the interests that they advance rather than the truths that they embody.

Underlying the theory is the contrast drawn by Marx (somewhat obscurely) between ideology and science. For Marx science is the opposite of ideology and also the cure for it. As we might put it now, scientific beliefs arise from and are explained by, the search for truth, and scientific method is the method by which we advance from truth to truth. Ideological beliefs arise from, and are explained by, the search for social and economic power. Hence we can criticize ideology from a scientific perspective, by showing that it is not a truth-seeking but a power-seeking device. But criticism of science from an ideological perspective is mere ideology, which explains and undermines nothing.

For Marx, the interests that are advanced by an ideology are those of a ruling class. We might similarly suggest that the interests advanced by totalitarian ideology are those of an aspiring elite. And we might confront totalitarian ideology in Marxian spirit, by explaining it in terms of its social function, and thereby exploding its epistemological claims. It is not the truth of Marxism that explains the willingness of intellectuals to believe it, but the power that it confers on intellectuals, in their attempts to control the world. And since, as Swift says, it is futile to reason someone out of a thing that he was not reasoned into, we can conclude that Marxism owes its remarkable power to survive every criticism to the fact that it is not a truth-directed but a power-directed system of thought.

That raises another question, which is *why* Marxism has this power – the power to confer power, to put it bluntly. Marxism conferred power on the intellectual elite because it placed something in their hands over and above a set of ideas and theories. What was that thing? And how could it be used to gain the rewards of government?

In answering that question we should also recall that Marxism was not the only totalitarian ideology of modern times. The ideology of the French revolutionaries was one of enlightened optimism, popular sovereignty and human rights; the ideology of the Nazis, although based on socialist theories, had an important racial and nationalist component that is alien to the central tenets of Marxism. All three ideologies, however, were adopted in the pursuit of power, and are to be explained in Marx's way, as power-seeking rather than truth-seeking devices. What is it, to repeat, that they placed in the hands of those who adopted them?

The answer to this question was suggested by Nietzsche. Totalitarian ideologies are ways to recruit resentment. Nietzsche used the French word *ressentiment*, in order to suggest a virulent and implacable state of mind, that precedes the injury complained of. Scheler, in his book on the subject, followed Nietzsche's usage.[77] Neither was discussing totalitarianism. Nietzsche was concerned to diagnose the evils, as he saw them, of Christianity; Scheler, who in my view entirely refutes Nietzsche's charge against the Christian faith, levels it, nevertheless, against the socialist doctrines of his time. In using the term 'resentment' I want to set myself at a distance from those controversies, and to use Nietzsche's suggestion for a purpose that he would perhaps not have recognized.

The picture I should like to urge is this. Totalitarian systems of government and totalitarian ideologies have a single source, which is resentment. I don't see resentment as Nietzsche saw it, as peculiar to the 'slave morality' of a Christian or post-Christian culture. I see it as an emotion that arises in all societies, being a natural offshoot of the competition for advantage. Totalitarian ideologies are adopted because they rationalize resentment, and also unite the resentful around a common cause. Totalitarian systems arise when the resentful, having seized power, proceed to abolish the institutions that have conferred power on others: institutions like law, property and religion which create hierar-

---

77   Nietzsche, *The Genealogy of Morals*, Part 1, section 8; Max Scheler, *Ressentiment*, trs. L. B. Coser and W. W. Holdheim, Milwaukee, WI: Marquette University Press, 1998.

chies, authorities and privileges, and which enable individuals to assert sovereignty over their own lives. To the resentful these institutions are the cause of inequality and therefore of their own humiliations and failures. In fact they are the channels through which resentment is drained away. Once institutions of law, property and religion are destroyed – and their destruction is the normal result of totalitarian government – resentment takes up its place immovably, as the ruling principle of the State.

For the resentful there is no such thing as real authority or legitimate power. There is only pure power, exercised by one person over another, and diagnosed through Lenin's famous questions: 'Who? Whom?'. Once in power, therefore, the resentful are inclined to dispense with mediating institutions, and erect a system of pure power relations, in which individual sovereignty is extinguished by central control. They may do this in the name of equality, meaning thereby to dispossess the rich and the privileged. Or they may do it in the name of racial purity, meaning thereby to dispossess the aliens who have stolen their birthright. One thing is certain, however, which is that there will be target groups. Resentment, in the form of it that I am considering, is not directed against specific individuals, in response to specific injuries. It is directed against groups, conceived as collectively offensive and bearing a collective guilt.

In every totalitarian experiment, therefore, you will find that the first act of the centralized power is to single out certain groups for punishment. The Jacobins targeted the aristocracy, later expanded to the ubiquitous 'emigrés', whose invisible presence licensed the most arbitrary murders and exterminations. The Nazis singled out the Jews, on account of their material success and because their apartness was both real and hidden. The Russian communists began with the bourgeoisie, but were fortunate in having to hand another and more artificial class of victim: the kulaks, a class created by the State, which could therefore easily be destroyed by the State. One function of the ideology is to tell an elaborate story about the target group, showing it to be less than human, unjustly successful and intrinsically worthy of punishment. Nothing is more comforting to the resentful than the thought that those who possess what they envy possess it unjustly. In the worldview of the resentful success is not a proof of virtue but, on the contrary, a call to retribution.

That explains why totalitarian ideologies invariably divide human beings into innocent and guilty groups. Behind the impassioned rhetoric of the *Communist Manifesto*, behind the pseudo-science of the labour theory of value, and behind the class analysis of human history, lies a single emotional source – resentment of those who control things. This resentment is both rationalized and amplified by the proof that property-owners form a 'class'. According to the theory the 'bourgeois' class has a shared moral identity, a shared and systematic access to the levers of power and a shared body of privileges. Moreover, all those good things are acquired and retained 'at the expense of', or through the 'exploitation' of, the proletariat, which has nothing to part with except its labour, and which will, therefore, always be cheated of what it deserves.

That theory has been effective not merely because it serves the function of amplifying and legitimizing resentment, but also because it is able to expose its rivals as 'mere ideology'. Here, I believe, is the most cunning feature of Marxist ideology: that it is able to pass itself off as science. Nazi genetics made a bid for the same high ground, but anti-Semitism was a social rather than a scientific outlook. The science supposedly gave support to the ideology; but it was not identical with it. The Jacobins also had scientific pretensions, but nothing, besides Enlightenment scepticism, with which to confront opposing views. In this respect Marx had the edge on his predecessors and his successors. Having hit on the distinction between ideology and science, he set out to prove that his own ideology was *in itself* a science. Moreover, Marx's alleged science undermined the beliefs of his opponents. The theories of the rule of law, the separation of powers, the right of property, and so on, as these had been expounded by 'bourgeois' thinkers like Montesquieu and Hegel, were shown, by the Marxian class analysis, to be not truth-seeking but power-seeking devices: ways of hanging on to the privileges conferred by the bourgeois order. By exposing this ideology as a self-serving pretence the class theory vindicated its own claims to scientific objectivity.

There is a kind of theological cunning in this aspect of Marx's thought. Since the class-theory is a genuine science, bourgeois political thought is ideology. And since the class-theory exposes bourgeois thought as ideology, it must be science. We have entered the magic circle of a creation myth. Moreover, by dressing up the theory in scientific language Marx has endowed it with the character of a badge of initiation. Not everybody can speak this language. A scientific theory defines the elite that can understand and apply it. It can offer proof of the elite's enlightened knowledge and therefore of its title to govern. It is this feature that justifies the charge made by Eric Voegelin, Alain Besançon and others that Marxism is a kind of gnosticism, a title to 'government through knowledge'.[78]

Here, then, is the perfect totalitarian ideology: a pseudo-science that justifies and recruits resentment, that undermines and dismisses all rival claims to legitimacy and that endows the not quite successful with the proof of their superior intellectual power and of their right to govern. The Marxian ideology provides the frustrated intellectual with the power that he needs: the power of his own resentment, which echoes and amplifies the resentment of a victim class.

It is a well-known fact[79] that revolutions are not conducted from below by the people, but from above, in the name of the people, by an aspiring elite. The French Revolution, for example, was the work of lawyers, professionals and minor nobility, impatient to enjoy political power in a society whose upper reaches were clogged up with functionless fat cats. The revolutionaries acted in the name of the people, announcing liberty, equality and fraternity. And they consciously identified themselves as an enlightened class, who had earned through their superior understanding the right to

---

78 See Eric Voegelin, *Science, Politics and Gnosticism*, Washington DC: Regnery Gateway, 1968; Alain Besançon, *The Intellectual Origins of Leninism*, tr. Sarah Matthews, Oxford: Blackwell, 1981.

79 Noticed at the outset of the French Revolution by Burke, later meditated upon by Tocqueville (*L'ancien régime et la Révolution*).

summon the people to their aid. Their slogans and doctrines did not merely legitimize their own resentment. They were calculated to conscript the resentment of others.

Now it is my contention that totalitarian ideologies always have that character. They legitimize the resentments of an elite, while recruiting the resentments of those needed to support the elite in its pursuit of hitherto inaccessible advantages. The elite derives its identity from repudiating the old order. And it casts itself in a pastoral role, as leader and teacher of the people. Its theories and visions have the status of revelations, conferring authority on the priestly caste. But they also identify a collective enemy, and in the destruction of this enemy the people can cheerfully join. The elite justifies its seizure of power by referring to its solidarity with those who have been unjustly excluded. Henceforth they will still be excluded, but *justly* – since they will be excluded in the name of the people, and therefore in the name of themselves.

We all feel resentment towards those whose success is either undeserved, or purchased at a cost to ourselves. There is nothing intrinsically evil in this, even if Christian morality urges us to forgive our enemies and to accept our humiliations in the sacrificial spirit of Christ. Indeed, some measure of resentment is necessary, if people are to keep a proper distance from each other and to treat strangers with respect. I am aware of the dangers of resentment, and therefore try to avoid provoking it. I give people their due, treat failure with sympathy, try to help those in need and do not make blatant display of my triumphs. In the words of Schoeck, I cultivate 'envy-avoiding' stratagems, knowing that I need strangers to accept my presence among them, and that I am as dependent upon their goodwill as they are on mine.[80] Resentment is the equilibrating device that keeps the society of strangers in balance, by punishing those who offend the laws of solidarity and rewarding, through its absence, those who contribute to the common good. Looked at with the superman superciliousness of

80   Helmut Schoeck, *Envy: A Theory of Social Behavior*, Indianapolis, IN: Liberty Fund, 1987.

Nietzsche resentment may seem like the bitter dregs of the 'slave morality', the impoverished loss of spirit that comes about when people take more pleasure in destroying others than in creating themselves. But that is the wrong way to look at it. Resentment is not a good thing to feel, either for its subject or its object. But the business of society is to conduct our social life so that resentment does not occur: to live by mutual aid and shared rejoicing, not so as to be all alike and inoffensively mediocre, but so as to gain the co-operation of others in our small successes. Living in this way we create the channels through which resentment drains away of its own accord: channels like custom, gift, hospitality and the common law, all of which are instantly stopped up when the totalitarians come to power. Resentment is to the body politic what pain is to the body: it is bad to feel it, but good to be capable of feeling it, since without the ability to feel it you will not survive.

Hence we should not resent the fact that we resent, but accept it, as a part of the human condition, something to be managed along with all our other joys and afflictions. However, resentment can be transformed into a governing emotion and a social cause, and thereby gain release from the constraints which normally contain it. This happens when resentment loses the specificity of its target, and becomes directed to society as a whole, and to the groups that are thought to control it. In such cases resentment ceases to be a response to another's unmerited success and becomes instead an existential posture: the posture of the one whom the world has betrayed, by first exciting and then denying his ambitions. This happens in many ways. For example, a person may be embittered by his small size, sexual failure and poor economic prospects, while at the same time nurturing energies and ambitions that promise the whole world as his rightful reward. And his bitterness may cause him to turn away from friends and to live in isolation. The result is a dangerous character, an unwanted by-product of the normal functioning of human society, and one who may seek some opportunity to take revenge on the world that has denied him his due. Such were St Just, Lenin and Hitler, and we know what they sought by way of compensation for their early failures. Such characters do not regard this person or that as the authors of their suffering. Their target is the human world as such. They are fired by a negative energy, and are never at ease unless bent on the task of destruction.

At the same time they seek a following, who will applaud them and reward them with gratitude, so compensating for their deep isolation. By gaining power they will also liberate their followers. Hence they must divide the world into the damned and the saved, the ones collectively responsible for the prevailing injustice and the ones who will be freed from their chains.

Imagine then what happens, when such a person decides to seek power. He will compensate for his isolation by establishing, in the place of friendship, a military command, with himself at the head of it. He will demand absolute loyalty and obedience, in return for a share in the reward. And he will admit no one into his circle who is not animated by resentment, which is the only emotion that he has learned to trust. His political project will not be to gain a share of power within existing structures, but to gain total power, so as to abolish the structures themselves. He will set himself against all forms of mediation, compromise and debate, and against the legal and moral norms which give a voice to the dissenter and sovereignty to the ordinary unresentful person. He will set about destroying the enemy, whom he will conceive in collective terms, as the class, group or race that hitherto controlled the world and which must now be controlled. And all institutions that grant protection to that class or a voice in the political process will be targets for his destructive rage.

The inevitable result of his seizure of power will be the establishment of a militarized core to the State – whether in the form of a party, a committee or simply an army which does not bother to disguise its military purpose. This core will have absolute power and will operate outside the law. The law itself will be replaced by a Potemkin version that can be invoked whenever it is necessary to remind the people of their subordinate position. This Potemkin law will not be a shy retreating thing, like law in civilized societies, which exists precisely in order to minimize its own invocation. It will be a prominent and omnipresent feature of society, constantly invoked and paraded, in order to imbue all acts of the ruling party with an unassailable air of legitimacy. The 'revolutionary vanguard' will be more prodigal of legal forms and official stamps than any of the regimes that it displaces, and the millions sent to their deaths will be granted an impeccable document to indicate that their end was rightfully decided and officially decreed. In this way the new order will be both utterly lawless and entirely concealed by law.[81]

The vanguard begins by targeting the culpable group, class or race. This will be a group marked by its previous success, the fruits of which will be taken from it and either destroyed or distributed among the victors. The members of the group will be humiliated and even reduced to some kind of animal condition, in order to display the extent of their former presumption. Hence the Gulag and the death camp arise naturally from the seizure of power, since they show the depth of the deceit that the world has hitherto practised against those who now control it. Resentment does not rest when its victim has been deprived of his worldly goods. It seeks to deprive him of his humanity, to show that he was never entitled to possess the slightest share in the Earth's resources and that his death is no more to be regretted than the death of any other kind of vermin. Exemplary in this respect was the humiliation of Marie Antoinette, Queen of France, who was accused of every crime, including incest, in order to represent her as excluded from the normal fold of humanity.

It is one mark of resentment in its pathological version that it will not allow a right of reply. The gap between accusation and guilt is closed. Hence the importance of the new and often invented crimes, which signify an existential condition rather than a specific act of wrongdoing. 'You are a Jew/bourgeois/kulak.' 'Well yes, I admit as much.' 'So what is your defence?'

However, the party that founds its rule on resentment will

---

81   Whittaker Chambers (*Witness*, 1952) made the same observation of the communist cells in America and elsewhere under Soviet orders. Any crime could be permitted: but the piece of paper and the rubber stamp were an integral part of it, there being no distinction, in the last analysis, between permission and command.

never feel at ease in the world that it creates. It will be like the puritan, as defined by H. L. Mencken, subject to 'the haunting fear that someone, somewhere, might be happy'. It will suspect that people are proceeding with the old way of life, expressing their energies, enjoying their successes, achieving the peace and happiness which the resentful are forever denied. The ruling party will tirelessly search for the weeds of human industry, the first frail tendrils of ownership, the timid attempts of people to grow together in their 'little platoons'. It will never be certain that the emigrés, Jews, bourgeoisie, kulaks or whoever have been finally destroyed, and will be haunted by the sense that for every one killed another comes to replace him. The order of resentment will be forced to confiscate not only the free economy but also the clubs, societies, schools and churches which have hitherto been the natural instruments of social reproduction. In short, resentment, once in power, will move of its own accord towards the totalitarian state.

Of course, the original resenters will die, most of them caught up in the machine that they made for others' destruction. One or two may even die from natural causes, though it is one of the pleasing lessons of recent history to discover how few they are. Eventually the machine will be functioning on automatic pilot, its software ossified into hardware. This is the final stage of totalitarianism – a stage not reached by the Jacobins or the Nazis, but reached in our day by the communists. In this condition, which Havel ventured to call 'post-totalitarian', the machine runs itself, fuelled by its own impersonal distillation of the original resentment. People learn to 'live within the lie' as Havel put it, and go about their daily betrayals with routine acquiescence, paying their debt to the machine and hoping that someone, somewhere, might know how to switch it off.[82]

The lesson that we should draw from the totalitarian movements of the twentieth century is that totalitarianism is not the natural form of a pathological outlook, but on the contrary the

---

82   Havel, 'The Power of the Powerless', in Jan Vladislav (ed.), *Václav Havel or Living in Truth*, London: Faber & Faber, 1987.

pathological form of a natural one. In normal people, who culti-vate the virtues of humility and live with their neighbours on good terms, resentment is a rare occurrence and one from which they can learn. It is stilled by compromise, and by the steady accu-mulation of social trust and collective knowledge that ensues when people live together by free association. But people who have an exaggerated sense of their own entitlements, and a diminutive capacity to deserve them, are apt to define themselves in opposition to that ordinary and neighbourly way of living with their fellow men. Their resentments are not concrete responses to momentary rebuffs but accumulating rejections of the system in which they have failed to advance. Intellectuals, it seems, are par-ticularly prone to this generalized resentment, even when they claim, like Nietzsche, to be free of it. Hence we should not be sur-prised to find intellectuals in the forefront of radical movements, or to discover that they are more disposed than ordinary mortals to adopt theories and ideologies that have nothing to recommend them apart from the power that they promise. Those who look back over the history of communism, and who take due note of what was written about it by Milosz in *The Captive Mind*, will recognize that there is at least a grain of truth in what I am trying to say. But they will be shocked, I think, to discover the extent to which the ideological journey of the Central European commu-nists is repeated by each generation of thinking people, even by those – especially by those – who enjoy the protection of wealthy universities and the privileges of a capitalist economy.

The process whereby resentment becomes detached from the institutions that normally defuse it, to become a generalized enmity, is familiar from another sphere: that of terrorism. The Russian Revolution was an outgrowth of the terrorist culture that had preceded it, and which had brought Russia to its knees. Observant writers at the time – Turgenev, Conrad, Dostoevsky – recognized the transformation of human character that ensues, when resentment gains the upper hand. Their portraits of the nihilists, terrorists and revolutionaries who destroyed the old world of Europe are of lasting significance, not least because they show the intricate psychological connection between the ideology of Marxism and the terrorism of the Marxist State. But the disappearance of totalitarian government does not mean the disappearance of resentment, nor the disappearance of the terrorist mentality. On the contrary, a new kind of stateless terror emerges, directed as before against the carefree and the successful and with only one goal, which is mass destruction. That is how we should understand al-Qa'eda: not as a religious movement but as a new kind of stateless terrorism, which has only the vaguest idea of what it wants to create, and a clear conception of what it wants to destroy.

9

Newspeak and Eurospeak

Social reality is malleable. How it is depends upon how it is perceived; and how it is perceived depends upon how it is described. Hence language is an important instrument in modern politics, and many of the political conflicts in our time are conflicts over words.

Perhaps the most obvious instance of this is provided by Soviet-style communism, and the invention of the language that we know, thanks to Orwell's *1984*, as Newspeak. Many of the terms of this language were taken from Marx; but they were grafted on to a native Russian habit of distinguishing things by their labels. Who and what am I? Who and what are you? Those are the questions that plagued the Russian romantics, and to which they produced answers that mean nothing in themselves, but which dictated the fate of those to whom they were applied. I am a member of the intelligentsia, you are a Narodnik; I am a nihilist, you are an anarchist; I am a progressive, you are a reactionary. What a gift to those 'beautiful souls', when the description 'communist' was offered on a plate, and with it a whole system of labels, by which to distinguish the good from the bad by the simple use of a word! Humanity, the Russian intelligentsia discovered, divides into classes – and what beautiful words, full of the sound of European culture, were used to describe them: bourgeoisie and proletariat; capitalist and socialist; exploiter and producer: and all with the simple and glorious meaning of them and us!

The course of communist politics should be understood in terms of the power of labels. Each of those who emerged triumphant from the Second International knew that he had been granted a vision that fully authorized his conduct. This Gnostic revelation was so clear that no argument was necessary, and no argument possible, that would provide it with a justifying proof. All that mattered was to distinguish those who shared the vision from those who dissented. And the most dangerous were those who dissented by so small a margin that they threatened to mingle their energies with yours, and so pollute the pure stream of action.

From the beginning, therefore, labels were required that would stigmatize the enemy within and justify his expulsion: he was a revisionist, a deviationist, an infantile leftist, a utopian socialist, a social fascist and so on. The original division between Menshevik and Bolshevik epitomized this process: those peculiar fabricated words, which were themselves crystallized lies, since the Mensheviks (minority) in fact composed the majority, were thereafter graven in the language of politics and in the motives of the communist elite. The success of these labels in marginalizing and condemning the opponent fortified the communist conviction that you could change reality by changing language. You could create a proletarian culture, just by inventing the word 'proletcult'. You could bring about the downfall of the free economy, simply by shouting 'crisis of capitalism' every time the subject arose. You could combine the absolute power of the Communist Party with the free consent of the people, by announcing communist rule as 'democratic centralism'.

How easy it proved, to murder millions of innocents, when nothing worse was occurring than 'the liquidation of the kulaks'. How simple a matter, to confine people for years in miserable camps, engaged in slave-labour until they sicken or die, if the only thing that language permits us to observe is 're-education'. The Nazis followed the example, and invented a Newspeak of their own. They learned that the silencing of opponents is not tyranny when described as *Gleichschaltung*, and that mass murder is no such thing when carried out as a 'final solution'.

Newspeak occurs whenever the main purpose of language – which is to describe reality – is replaced by the rival purpose of asserting power over it. The fundamental speech-act is only superficially represented by the assertoric grammar. Newspeak sentences sound like assertions, but their underlying logic is the logic of the spell. They show the triumph of words over things, the futility of rational argument and also the danger of resistance. As a result Newspeak developed its own special syntax which – while closely related to the syntax deployed in ordinary descriptions – carefully avoids any encounter with reality or any exposure to the logic of rational argument. This Françoise Thom has tried to show in her brilliant study, *La langue de bois*.[83] I will be taking her argument forward by considering another and newer kind of 'langue de bois', namely that which has emerged with the European Union, and which has become the official language of the Commission. The purpose of communist Newspeak, in Françoise Thom's ironical words, was 'to protect ideology from the malicious attacks of real things'. The purpose of Eurospeak is not to protect an ideology, but to protect a system of privileges. Hence the underlying logic is not that of the spell but that of the mystery, in which challenging questions are finally shown to be unanswerable, and therefore unaskable. At the same time, like Newspeak, Eurospeak exemplifies an evasiveness towards rational argument, and an intolerance towards any opposition to the fundamental agenda.

The distinction between Newspeak and Eurospeak can be grasped through an example of each. The Newspeak term 'capitalism', which has entered the language in another sense, refers strictly to the system mythopoeically described in *Das Kapital* – in other words to a system of economic control in which private property is all in the hands of a non-producing 'bourgeois' class. Used in such phrases as 'the crisis of capitalism', 'capitalist exploitation', 'capitalist ideology' and so on, the term functions as a kind of spell, the equivalent in economic theory of Khrushchev's great scream from the rostrum of the United

---

83 Françoise Thom, *La langue de bois*, Paris: Julliard, 1987, tr. C. Janson, *Newspeak*, London: Claridge Press, 1985.

Nations: 'We will bury you!' By describing free economies with this term, Newspeak casts the spell that extinguishes them. The reality of the free economy disappears behind the description, to be replaced by a strange baroque edifice, constantly falling to the ground in a dream-sequence of ruin.

This is not to say that there is not a perfectly serious use of the term 'capitalism' in economic theory. We can disagree with the central argument put forward by Marx in *Das Kapital*, while accepting that there is such a thing as economic capital, and such a thing as its private deployment. And we might describe an economy in which substantial capital is in the hands of private individuals as capitalist, meaning that term as a neutral description that may or may not, in due course, form part of a theory that uncovers the truth. But that is not how the term is used in Newspeak, which has no place for neutral descriptions and should be understood as a defence against truth, rather than a means to embrace it.

We should here compare the Eurospeak term 'subsidiarity'. This term, too, has a legitimate use. When embedded in Eurospeak, however, 'subsidiarity' loses its referential character, in just the way that 'capitalism' loses its referential character in Newspeak. Encountering the term 'subsidiarity' in the documents of the EU you enter the vicinity of a mystery, from which you are expected to learn only one thing, which is that enquiry is futile. The term invariably occurs in the vicinity of a seriously damaging question, namely: what remains of the democratic forms of government achieved by the nation states, when the EU takes charge of their legislation? The answer is that we must apply the 'principle of subsidiarity', according to which decisions are all to be taken at the 'lowest level compatible with the project of Union'. 'What is this lowest level?' you may ask, and 'Who decides which decisions are to be taken there?' The only possible answer to the second of those questions – namely, 'the EU apparatus, including the European Court of Justice' – removes all meaning from the first. To say that the nation states have sovereignty in all matters that they are competent to decide, but that the EU apparatus decides which matters those are, is to say that the nation states have no sovereignty at all, since all their powers are delegated. In other words 'subsidiarity' effectively removes the sovereignty that it purports to grant, and so wraps the whole idea of sovereignty in an impenetrable cloud of mystery. True, the EU Constitutional Treaty incorporated a protocol reaffirming the principle of subsidiarity, and requiring EU institutions to show evidence, before taking charge of some matter, that it cannot be dealt with at the national level. But the standard of proof is vague, and the arbiter appointed is the European Court of Justice, an institution committed to the project of 'ever closer union', under whose jurisdiction the *acquis communautaire* has already expanded to 97,000 pages. Hence the protocol again merely removes the guarantees that it purports to grant.

As I said, however, the term 'subsidiarity' has a legitimate use, describing a form of organization recommended by the social doctrine of the Catholic Church and elevated to a principle of government in a papal encyclical of Pius XI in 1931. From this source it was appropriated by Wilhelm Röpke, in his effort to develop a social and political theory in which the market economy would be reconciled with local community and the 'little platoon'.[84] What Röpke meant, and what Catholic doctrine implied, was very different from anything that could be expressed in Eurospeak. Subsidiarity, in Röpke's understanding of the term, refers to the absolute right of local communities to take decisions for themselves, including the decision to surrender the matter to a larger forum. Subsidiarity places an absolute brake upon centralizing powers, by permitting their involvement only when requested. In Eurospeak, however, 'subsidiarity' has the opposite sense, providing a comprehensive authorization to the EU institutions, to expropriate whatever powers they might deem to be theirs. By purporting to grant powers in the very word that removes them, the EU constitution wraps the whole idea of decentralized government in mystery. A similar mystery is enshrined in such words as 'proportionality', 'solidarity', 'ever

---

84 Wilhelm Röpke, *A Humane Economy*, tr. Elizabeth Henderson, Chicago: Henry Regnery, 1960.

closer union' and *'acquis communautaire'*: words and phrases which suggest a popular process of lawful gain, but whose real meaning is loss. To say that a power has become part of the *acquis communautaire*, for example, is not to say that it has been acquired by anything, or is henceforth to be exercised by any accountable body. It is to say that it has been lost in the bureaucratic labyrinth, so that nobody henceforth will really know how it is deployed, or how to rectify the abuse of it.

Just as Newspeak describes an embattled world, in which the forces of progress are constantly called upon to defeat the malignant 'isms' that threaten them – capitalism, imperialism, left deviationism and so on – so does Eurospeak fill the world with its own brand of dangerous 'isms', abstract forces which are also mysteries at least as unfathomable as the 'ever closer union' that they threaten. Chief of these mysterious 'isms' is the 'racism and xenophobia' against which we are warned by the Commission in one after another of its official pronouncements and directives, and which has now been made into a crime. Nobody knows what this crime involves – and that is the real purpose of the label, namely, to instil in the public mind the idea of a malign force that stalks through all European society, inhabiting the hearts and brains of people who may not be aware of its machinations, diverting even the most innocent project on to the path of sin. My own very English patriotism might be a proof of guilt; in declaring myself the enemy of Eurospeak it is possible that I am exhibiting xenophobia; my Anglo-Saxon culture could very well convict me of racism. Or maybe not. How am I to know? The important point is that I am not to know. I am to remain baffled by the mysterious possibility of my own criminal frame of mind, so as to learn not to question the wise decrees by which I am henceforth to be governed. Racism and xenophobia are strictly thought-crimes, of the kind described by Orwell.

The contrast between Newspeak, as a system of spells, and Eurospeak, as a system of mysteries, should not blind us to the very important syntactical similarities between them, and especially to the way in which the underlying message is in each case encoded. Some of the syntactical peculiarities have been noted by

Françoise Thom: the use of nominalizations instead of direct verbs, the lack of indexicals, the preference for the passive voice and impersonal idioms, the replacement of predications with comparatives, the ubiquitous imperative mood. To some extent these features are exhibited by all uses of language in which the speaker is attempting to avoid liability for what he says, or to justify as an ineluctable necessity what he wishes to impose as a decree. Hence all bureaucracies tend to express themselves in wooden language. Here is an example involving all the features noted by Professor Thom:

> The development of the productive forces brought about by the ever more scientific use of labour power has prepared the way for the new five-year plan, whose launch is an imperative necessity.

Nobody is really identified as the subject of that sentence; the crucial verb ('to develop') has been nominalized and ossified; indexicals like 'I', 'we', 'here' and 'now' have been eliminated; the reference to scientific uses of labour-power has been muddled by a comparative ('ever more scientific use' – ever more than what?); all concrete action has been hidden within the passive voice ('brought about by'); and the whole moves towards a vague but inescapable imperative, addressed to no one in particular, and therefore to everyone in general. The blocks of abstract terms serve the function of concealing all concrete difficulties, while authorizing whatever forms of coercion might seem necessary to those charged with implementing the new five-year plan. Professor Thom gives sufficient examples of these devices in Newspeak to convince the reader that they are not accidental, but the necessary result of the underlying aim – the aim of safeguarding ideology from the malicious assaults of reality.

The features described by Professor Thom are not merely syntactical. For syntax, here as elsewhere, reflects semantics; it exists in order to convey a particular meaning – to cast a spell, as in communist Newspeak, or to envelop a bureaucratic project in protective mystery, as in Eurospeak. The elimination of indexicals, the passive voice, and the nominalizations are all part of a single project, which is to remove the human individual and his choices from the subject-matter of politics. The human individual is the single most important obstacle that all bureaucratic systems must overcome, and which all ideologies must destroy. His attachment to particulars and contingencies; his embarrassing tendency to reject what has been devised for his betterment; his freedom of choice and the rights and duties through which he exercises it – all these are obstacles to the conscientious bureaucrat, as he strives to implement his five-year plan. Hence the need to phrase political choice in such a way that individuals have no part in it. Newspeak prefers to speak of forces, classes and the march of history, and regards the actions of Great Men as acceptable subjects for discussion only because Great Men, like Napoleon, Lenin and Hitler, are really the expression of abstract forces, such as imperialism, revolutionary socialism and fascism. The 'isms' that govern political change work *through* people, but not *from* them.

Connected with the relentless use of abstractions is the feature that Thom describes as 'pan-dynamism'. The world of Newspeak is a world of abstract forces, in which individuals are merely local embodiments of the 'isms' that are revealed in them; hence it is a world without action. However, it is not a world without movement. On the contrary, everything is in constant motion, swept onwards by the forces of progress, or impeded by the forces of reaction. There is no equilibrium, no stasis, no rest in the world of Newspeak. All stillness is a deception, the quietus of a volcano that could erupt at any time. This feature of Newspeak was particularly apparent during the 'peace offensive' that followed the Soviet invasion of Afghanistan, when Soviet propaganda, acting in conjunction with peace movements in the West, resurrected the 'struggle for peace' of the Cold War. Peace never appears in Newspeak as a condition of rest and normality. It is always something to 'fight for', and 'Fight for Peace!', 'Struggle for Peace!' took their place among the official slogans of the party.

From the same source comes the penchant of Newspeak for 'irreversible' changes. Since everything is in motion and the 'struggle' between the forces of progress and the forces of reaction is always and everywhere, it is important that the triumph of ideology over reality be constantly recorded and endorsed. Hence progressive forces always achieve 'irreversible changes', while reactionary forces are wrong-footed by their contradictory and merely 'nostalgic' attempts to defend a doomed social order.

Eurospeak mirrors this feature of Newspeak. It eschews the repeated reference to fight, struggle and conflict. But it pins its exhortations to a pan-dynamic vision of the political process, in which all 'positive' changes are irreversible, and all negative changes merely temporary set-backs, caused by racism, xenophobia, Little Englandism, nationalism and so on. This explains the preference for comparatives noted earlier. Just as the official announcements of Newspeak refer to ever more 'scientific', progressive or productive initiatives, without ever specifying just what point on the scale of science, progress or production we have reached, so does Eurospeak build itself around a project of 'ever closer union', without pausing to consider how much union has so far been attained or how much union would be desirable. Everything is constantly moving forwards along the single path, and while sometimes Eurospeak will refer to a 'fast track' and a 'slow track' into the future, the tracks lead in the same direction, which is nowhere definite, since it can be described only in comparative terms.

Thus the constitutional treaty (not adopted, but not abandoned either) begins with the phrase: 'The peoples of Europe, in creating an ever closer union among them, are resolved . . .'. No one had ever asked the peoples of Europe whether they wanted an 'ever closer union', or what they understand the phrase to mean. Nevertheless, it seems that the peoples of Europe are moving of their own accord in this direction, and have made resolutions accordingly. Everything thereafter is infected by the pan-dynamism of this opening phrase. We are exhorted not to respect rights but to 'strengthen rights in light of social progress', not to co-operate but 'to work towards developing a coordinated strategy'. Instead of making adjustments the union is to 'develop and pursue its action leading to the strengthening of its economic, social and

territorial cohesion'. Those vague phrases could not possibly
form the basis of a constitution in the Anglo-Saxon understanding of the term, since they are without clear legal force, and
depend for their interpretation on a political project rather than a
legal ruling.

It is interesting to note that Newspeak does not require com-
placent acceptance of the official line. On the contrary, you can
use it to make the most devastating criticisms of the power that
speaks through it, without risking censure. Conversely, you can
praise that power in terms not authorized by Newspeak, and find
yourself in serious trouble. Suppose a Czech were to have
responded to the Soviet invasion of his country with the following
sentence:

> The fraternal assistance offered to the progressive forces in
> our country liquidated strata of the bourgeois class that
> might otherwise have been compelled to contribute to the
> ever more scientifically founded development of society.

In plain language that says that the Soviet invasion destroyed
those with the knowledge needed by modern government. But it is
phrased in such a way as to protect the speaker from adverse criticism, and to neutralize the import of what he says. The vocabulary and syntax affirm what the underlying thought denies, and in
the contest between them it is the thought that is defeated.

Suppose on the other hand the Czech citizen had welcomed the
invasion in the following words:

> The invasion by the Warsaw Pact armies was successful in
> destroying popular protest against Communist Party rule,
> and in re-establishing the Communist Party as the supreme
> authority in the state.

Those are dangerous words, and anyone who uttered them would
risk punishment. Although the speaker praises the Soviet strategy
by accurately describing its success, his vocabulary and syntax
reveal a soul that has not replaced truth by correctness, reality by

ideology. The point is that you can disagree with everything that the party says and does, provided that you do so in the party's language – for the purpose of that language is to make agreement and disagreement, belief and doubt, truth and falsehood indistinguishable. Newspeak cancels reality, even in the act of describing it.

Now I don't say that Eurospeak is so radical in its effect. Nevertheless, it is also in the business of preventing discussion. Concealed within the crucial phrases – *ever closer union, subsidiarity, solidarity, proportionality*, etc. – is the non-negotiable appropriation of powers by an unaccountable body. Like the Communist Party, this body is defined by an unchangeable agenda, and depends upon no individual human being for its continuity. The only thing that can alter its agenda or bring its machinations to an end is a concerted effort of free discussion, leading to a widespread resistance to the ruling schemes. By offering indecipherable mysteries at all the points where discussion might lead to a rejection of the agenda, Eurospeak protects the privileges of the Eurocrats as effectively as Newspeak protected the power of the communists.

In understanding the working of bureaucracies we must take account of the ideological climate in which they operate. This climate is like the climate of a rain forest: both the product and the producer of the growth that it surrounds. Bureaucracies are instances of a general phenomenon identified and analysed by James Buchanan and the 'Virginia school' of economists: the phenomenon of 'rent-seeking', meaning the process whereby people can claim a rent on economic activities which they do not themselves engage in – in particular by lobbying and legislation that diverts resources to the bureaucracy, while contributing nothing to the productive process. The EU has been set up in such a way that the rents are enormous and the risks non-existent, so long as the project endures – hence the need to describe the project in the pan-dynamic terms discussed above, as a project without an end. People who secure rents in such a system form a natural 'interest group', whose principal concern will be to maximize the resources turned in their direction, and to ensure security of tenure for each of their members.

Interest groups generate and thrive upon ideologies. Ideological beliefs tend to declare a separation between 'us' and 'them': they offer a criterion of membership, which reinforces the unity of the group, while providing a barrier to entry from outside. An interest group united by an ideology has a much better chance of gaining control of a rent, for the reason that its members will be less likely to compete with each other in the pursuit of it, and more likely to unite against outside rivals. This effect is enhanced, paradoxically, by an ideology of 'inclusion': the bureaucrat who is overseeing a system that ostensibly excludes no one from its benefits can easily justify the exclusive privileges that he himself enjoys. This trick was perfected by the Communist Party, which loudly condemned all privileges and distinctions, while rigorously excluding anyone who might jeopardize the privileges bestowed on its members. (Hence the ideological witch-hunts, and the constant return to a 'correctness' that the party alone was authorized to define.) All European documents, therefore, including the Constitution, contain gestures towards an 'inclusive' ideology, and this ideology will gradually exert a controlling influence over regulation. Not that regulation will actually achieve the goal of 'social inclusion': for, like all technicalities of Eurospeak, this term denotes a mystery that cannot be unravelled. The point is that measures must pass an ideological test. As long as the phrase 'social inclusion' can be uttered over them, regulations will be blessed and protests will condemn themselves as politically 'incorrect'. The function of the 'inclusive' ideology is not to include anyone, but to exclude those who pose a threat to the new political class. Hence the fate of Sr Rocco Buttiglione, thrown off the gravy train for his orthodox Christian beliefs.

It might be objected that every bureaucracy needs a codified language, that the features of Newspeak and Eurospeak that I have discussed are merely stylistic, and that the abuses that they may seem to authorize stem not from the language but from the people who use it. In conclusion I shall reply to that objection, and in the course of doing so suggest a theory of natural political language.

Newspeak and Eurospeak are certainly bureaucratic idiolects.

Their distinguishing feature, however, is that they derive from a comprehensive plan, and a plan that has no defined goal – or a goal defined so vaguely that nobody really knows what it is or how to achieve it. Communism defined the goal as 'full communism', relying on the theory of Marx to permit its indefinite postponement. The EU defines the goal as union, but avoids concrete specifications as to what union consists in, relying instead on the idea that we are always getting closer to it, while never actually achieving it. It is such plans that produce the distortions of the *langue de bois*. When people wish to plan for humanity, they cannot allow human life to take its natural course, since that is a course inimical to comprehensive planning. The concepts that arise in normal dialogue arise from the need to compromise, to reach agreements, to establish peaceful co-ordination with people who do not share your projects or your affections, but who are as much in need of space as you are. Such concepts have little or nothing to do with the schemes and plans of the bureaucrat, since they permit those who use them to change course, to drop one goal and pick up another, to amend their ways and to show infinite flexibility.

The intellectual in his garret can contemplate with satisfaction and a clear conscience the 'liquidation of the bourgeoisie'. But when he enters the shop downstairs he must speak another language. Only in the most distant sense is this man behind the counter a member of the bourgeoisie. If I choose, nevertheless, so to see him it is because I am using the word 'bourgeois' as part of a spell – I am trying to gain power over this person through labelling him. In confronting the shopkeeper as a human being I must renounce this presumptuous bid for power, and accord to him a voice of his own. My language must make room for his voice, and that means it must be shaped to permit the resolution of conflict, the forging of agreement, including the agreement to differ. I make remarks about the weather, grumble about politics, 'pass the time of day' – and my language has the effect of softening reality, of making it pliable and serviceable. Newspeak, which denies reality, also hardens it, by turning it into something alien and resistant, a thing to be 'struggled with' and 'overcome'.

Hayek would describe the ordinary quotidian discourse between the shopkeeper and me as 'catallactic': a matter of individual exchange rather than the imposition of a plan. Catallactic discourse generates social relations not by a plan but by an 'invisible hand'. I may have come down from my garret with a plan in view, intending the first move towards the liquidation of the bourgeoisie about which I had read in my Marxist textbook. But this plan will not survive the first exchange of words with my chosen victim, and the attempt to impose it or to speak the language that announces it will have the same effect as the wind in Aesop's fable, competing with the sun to remove the coat of a traveller. Ordinary language warms and softens; Newspeak freezes and hardens. And ordinary discourse generates out of its own resources the concepts that Newspeak forbids: fair/unfair; just/unjust; honest/dishonest; yours/mine. Such concepts, which belong to the free exchange of feelings, opinions and goods, also, when freely expressed and acted upon, create a society in which order is spontaneous and not planned. Newspeak does not merely impose a plan; it also eliminates the discourse through which human beings can live without one. If justice is referred to in Newspeak, it is not the justice of individual dealings, but 'social justice', the kind of 'justice' imposed by a plan, which invariably involves treating individuals unjustly, by depriving them of their freedom, their home and their goods.

Ever since the Enlightenment thinkers have been tempted by the idea of a planned society, and as a result have tended to lose sight of the fact that real social discourse arises from encounters between individuals, being part of day-to-day problem-solving and the minute search for agreement. Real social discourse veers away from 'irreversible changes', regards all arrangements as adjustable and allows a voice to all those whose agreement it seeks. From just the same source stems the English common law and the parliamentary institutions that have embodied the sovereignty of the British people. This is why the British react far more unfavourably than other Europeans to the great Euro-plan. They sense its encroachment, not merely on their legislative sovereignty, but also on the very language with which law and politics are conducted. Eurocrats who justify their decisions in terms of 'proportionality and subsidiarity', who propose laws for 'the next stage of European construction', who restrict freedoms in the name of 'the precautionary principle' appear, to one used to speaking the language of common-law justice, like alien monsters, who have fallen out of communication with human kind. Their legislative proposals have the same threatening air as proposals announced in Newspeak, and the impossibility of replying to or amending them is contained in the very language in which they are framed. How can you show that a proposal does not respect the requirements of proportionality or subsidiarity, when the right to determine the meaning of these terms has been expropriated by a court that has no interest in doing any such thing? How can you show that your proposals do not violate the 'precautionary principle', when nobody has shown the slightest ability or willingness to tell us what the principle says?[85] Eurospeak is directed against the catallactic sovereignty that arises by proximity and agreement. It re-describes the social world as a dynamic process, led by a vanguard class of bureaucrats, proceeding inexorably but asymptotically towards its goal. The lesson of recent history is that, if you describe the world in this way, you may also change it – though probably not in the way you intend. Planning on this scale can succeed only by some kind of unforeseeable accident. The gravy train can certainly be sent speeding into the future; but what kind of crash awaits it is anyone's guess.

---

85   See R. Scruton, 'The Cult of Precaution', in *The National Interest*, no. 76, Summer 2004, pp. 148–54.

10

The Nature of Evil

The suffering caused by an earthquake may be far greater than the suffering caused by a terrorist bomb. But terrorism, unlike earthquakes, is a form of evil. There are evil deeds, evil thoughts, evil desires and evil people: but states of affairs can be evil only if someone can be blamed for them. And the evil resides in the person blamed. As Kant put it, '*good* or *evil* always implies a reference to the *will*' (*Critique of Practical Reason*, ch. 2). At the same time, we distinguish people who are evil from those who are merely bad. The bad person is like you or me, only worse. He belongs in the community, even if he behaves badly towards it. We can reason with him, improve him, come to terms with him and, in the end, accept him. He is made, like us, from the 'crooked timber of humanity'.

There is a certain kind of person who is bad but not bad in that simple and comprehensible way – and he provides a paradigm of evil, and a justification for our use of the word. The kind of person I have in mind is one who does not belong in the community, even if he resides within its territory. His bad behaviour may be too secret and subversive to be noticeable, and any dialogue with him will be, on his part, a pretence. There is, in him, no scope for improvement, no path to acceptance, and even if we think of him as human, his faults are not of the normal, remediable, human variety, but have another and more metaphysical origin. He is a visitor from another sphere, an incarnation of the Devil. Even his charm – and it is a recognized fact that evil people are often charming – is only further proof of his Otherness. He is, in some sense, the negation of humanity, wholly and unnaturally at ease with the thing that he seeks to destroy.

That characterization of evil is summarized in the famous line that Goethe gives to Mephistopheles:

> *Ich bin der Geist der stets verneint* (I am the spirit that forever negates).

Whereas the bad person is guided by self-interest, to the point of ignoring or overriding the others who stand in his path, the evil person is profoundly interested in others, has almost selfless designs on them. His aim is not to use them, as Faust uses Gretchen, but to rob them of themselves. Mephistopheles hopes to steal and destroy Faust's soul and, en route to that end, to destroy the soul of Gretchen. Nowadays, we might use the word 'self' instead of 'soul', in order to avoid religious connotations. But this word is only another name for the same deep metaphysical mystery around which our lives are built – the mystery of individual freedom. The evil person is not necessarily a threat to your body; but he is a threat to your self.

We should not be surprised to find, therefore, that evil people are often opaque to us. However lucid their thoughts, however transparent their deeds, their motives are somehow uncanny, inexplicable, like intrusions from another realm of causality. We make sense of Mephistopheles because he is a visitor from that other realm, whose affability and charm do not disguise the inner torment. But when it comes to Iago, for example, the villain of Shakespeare's play *Othello*, we are puzzled. Through his words and deeds Iago prompts the stunned recognition that he really means to destroy Othello, that there is no sufficient motive apart from the desire to do this terrible thing, and that there is no plea or reasoning that could deflect him from his path.

Boïto, in his libretto for Verdi's *Otello*, provides Iago with a celebrated 'negative confession', in order to give credibility to the metaphysical nature of his desires. But Shakespeare gives us no such assistance. He vaguely hints, here and there, at jealousy, while making clear that this jealousy falls far short of explaining the concentrated malice aimed at Othello. After all, Iago seeks to destroy Othello by causing Othello to destroy Desdemona, who has done Iago no wrong. It is the incomprehensible, as it were *noumenal*, nature of Iago's motive that enables him so effectively to conceal it. Peering into Iago's soul we find a void, a nothingness; like Mephistopheles, he is a great negation, a soul composed of anti-spirit, as a body might be composed of anti-matter.

In referring to the metaphysical nature of the evil motive I am not using a metaphor. But nor am I suggesting any particular metaphysical theory. Rather, I am pointing to the way in which we conceptualize evil. It does not follow from our habit of describing evil people in this way that we believe them to be supernatural, or outside the chain of physical causality. The problem posed by the existence of evil people, as I understand it, is not very different from the problem of freedom: indeed, it is a part of it. You can believe that we human beings are free, that freedom is a distinct metaphysical condition, and that nevertheless we are as much a part of the natural order as everything else. This set of beliefs is puzzling, and only certain metaphysical theories will render it consistent. But the puzzle does not derive from a metaphysical *theory*. It derives from a metaphysical *concept* – that of freedom – which is forced on us by the attempt to describe things as they seem. Whether things *are* as they seem is of course one part of the philosophical problem.

The same is true, I hold, of evil. And if we were to conclude that there is no way of making sense of evil without the use of theological notions, then this would be an argument for thinking that those notions are not as empty as some people think them to be. For evil exists, and if we can understand this fact only on the assumption of some theological premise, then we have a reason for thinking that premise to be true.

There are, to my knowledge, no truly evil people in classical literature. Homer invents terrors like Circe and the Cyclops, but is unacquainted with the kind of desire to destroy another person that we witness in Iago. The tragedians treat of murderous frenzy and divine madness. But even in Medea or Clytemnestra the fury enters the soul from outside, and possession is wholly explicable in terms of personal trauma.[86]

Medieval literature, for all its belief in the Devil and his works, treats people with a kind of burlesque familiarity that bears little or no relation to the witch-hunts and millenarian furies that ravaged the medieval world. The inhabitants of Dante's *Inferno* are noteworthy for their humanity, and for faults with which all of us can at some level identify. They suffer, surrounded by terrors. But the negative energy of a Mephistopheles seems to have no real place in their emotions. In English literature it was perhaps Shakespeare who first came to grips with evil as a distinct spiritual condition, and although the Jacobean tragedians (Ford and Webster in particular) followed in Shakespeare's footsteps, they added to his account less substance than melodrama. Webster's 'White Devil' seems, when set beside Iago, merely unmotivated, rather than motivated in a mysterious and meta-physical way. As for Milton's Satan, it has been frequently observed that he is, in a sense, the most admirable person in *Paradise Lost*, almost noble in his implacable resentment and in his refusal to be cowed.[87]

Nor do we encounter the demonic power of Shakespeare's Iago in many novels: perhaps in Valmont and Mme de Merteuil in Laclos's *Les Liaisons dangereuses*, and perhaps in Richardson's Lovelace in *Clarissa*. Hardy's Alec D'Urbeville has a part of evil, as does Balzac's Cousine Bette. But such modern characters seem not to cross the gulf from physical to metaphysical motives. Only here and there – notably in Dostoevsky (in Smerdyakov and Karamazov *père*, for instance, or in the nihilistic hooligans of *The Possessed*) – do we find, in nineteenth-century novels, that pure,

---

86 See Ruth Padel, *Whom Gods Destroy*, Princeton: Princeton University Press, 1995. Padel's account of tragedy is based on her subtle analysis of the implicit theory of the mind that is assumed by the tragedians: see *In and Out of the Mind: Greek Images of the Tragic Self*, Princeton: Princeton University Press, 1992.

87 Such is the view defended, for example, by William Empson in *Milton's God*, London: Chatto and Windus, 1961, and to a measure endorsed by Christopher Ricks in *Milton's Grand Style*, Oxford: Clarendon Press, 1963.

almost disinterested, need for moral destruction that pervades the spirit of Iago.

In short, the evil person is not a familiar figure in our literature, and when we encounter him in life he fills us with a sense of the uncanny. He is like a fracture in our human world, through which we catch glimpses of the void. And here, it seems to me, is one explanation of the phenomenon summed up by Hannah Arendt in the phrase 'the banality of evil'.[88] The terrible destruction that has been wrought, and deliberately wrought, on human beings in recent times, in the name of this or that political ideology, has not typically been wrought by evil people. Eichmann was no Iago, but an ordinary official – a bad man, certainly, but not one driven by some metaphysical antipathy to the human soul. He was a bureaucrat, given to obeying orders, and willing to sacrifice his conscience to his own security when the time to disobey had come. The torture, degradation and death that it was his role to oversee were not, in his eyes, his doing, but the inevitable effects of a machine that had been set in motion without his help. Evil occurred around him but, in his own eyes, it was not something that he did.

Of course, we repudiate Eichmann's excuses, and hold him answerable for the suffering that he might – at a cost – have remedied. We recognize that the death camp was not just a bad thing that happened, but an evil that was done. And Eichmann was implicated in this evil. As Arendt also points out, the camps were designed not merely to destroy human beings but also to deprive them of their humanity. The inmates were to be treated as things, humiliated, degraded, reduced to a condition of bare, unsupported and all-consuming need, which would cancel in them the last vestiges of freedom. In other words the goal included that pursued in one way by Iago and in another way by Mephistopheles, which was to rob the inmates of their souls. The camps were animated by anti-spirit, and people caught up in them stumbled around as though burdened by a great negation sign. These anti-humans were repulsive and verminous

---

88　Hannah Arendt, *Eichmann in Jerusalem*, New York: Viking Press, 1963.

to those permitted to observe them. Hence their extermination could be represented as necessary, and their disappearance into a shared forgetfulness became the spiritual equivalent of matter tumbling into a black hole.

We should not understand the camps, therefore, as dreadful in the way that an earthquake, a forest fire or a famine are dreadful, even though these natural disasters may produce suffering on just as great a scale. The camps did not exist to produce suffering only; they were designed to eradicate the humanity of their victims. They constituted a gesture of defiance towards the Creator, displaying the emptiness and worthlessness of his promises. Once the soul was destroyed destruction of the body would not be perceived as murder, but only as a kind of pest control. And I would identify this as a paradigm of evil: namely, the attempt or desire to destroy the soul of another, so that his value and meaning are rubbed out. Thus the torturer wishes the will, freedom, conscience and integrity of his victim to be destroyed by pain, in order to relish the sight of what Sartre tellingly describes as 'freedom abjured'.[89] In other words, he is using the body to destroy the soul, and delighting in the ruin and humiliation that he can bring about through pain. But pain is not the only means to this goal; nor is it always the most effective.

I have described the death camps in terms of a purpose. But whose purpose, exactly? This question brings us face to face with another of the mysteries of evil, and it is one that has exercised many writers in recent times, from Orwell to Solzhenitsyn. Ask of any individual, whether he or she intended the degradation of the death camps, and often it is hard to find an answer. Of course, many of the Nazi leaders did intend some such thing, since they were animated by a hatred that demanded the extremes of mal-treatment. In the Soviet case, however, the camps continued long after the death of Lenin, Stalin and their entourage, when nobody existed who had ever intended this result, when possibly even those involved in overseeing the system regretted its existence and

---

89   Jean-Paul Sartre, *L'Etre et le néant*, Paris: Gallimard, 1943, tr. Hazel E. Barnes, London: Methuen, 1957, p. 404.

when nobody who made the crucial decisions saw himself as anything but a helpless cog in the machine.[90]

Orwell presents the 'Ideal Type' of this situation in *1984*. Who among the protagonists in that novel knows whether Big Brother really exists? Who in the system is giving orders, rather than receiving them and passing them on? Orwell has imagined a situation in which evil arises, so to speak, 'by an invisible hand' from the multitudinous deals that are needed for survival. And the mechanism that yields this result is itself the outcome of an invisible hand – beginning perhaps from genuinely evil intentions, but maintained in being by the same 'banality' that Arendt discerned in the motives of Adolf Eichmann.

As we know, Orwell was inspired to write *1984* as a result of observing the conduct of the communists in the Spanish civil war. He certainly believed that those people were acting with evil intentions. But he also recognized that they were part of a machine that would guarantee a dreadful outcome, whatever the intentions of those who operated it. And his judgement in the matter has been confirmed by countless subsequent observers of the communist system, from Milosz and Koestler to Solzhenitsyn, Havel and Kolakowski.[91] The question that those writers raise still troubles us: to whom should this evil be imputed? Is it not conceivable that it should have arisen *even from the best of intentions*? And if that is so, whence does it come? *Unde malum?* To say that it comes from no intention or purpose, that it is really a mistake or a misfortune rather than a crime, is precisely to deny that it is evil.

In a study of Orwell's *1984* Alain Besançon argues that the totalitarian society envisaged by Orwell can be understood only in theological terms.[92] For it is a society founded on a transcen-

90   Anne Applebaum, *Gulag*, New York: Doubleday, 2003.
91   Czeslaw Milosz, *The Captive Mind*, tr. June Zielonko, London: Faber & Faber, 1953; Václav Havel, 'The Power of the Powerless', in *Václav Havel or Living in Truth*, op. cit.; Leszek Kolakowski, *Main Currents of Marxism*, vol. 3, Oxford: OUP, 1978.
92   Alain Besançon, *La Falsification du bien*, Paris 1988, tr. Matthew Screech, *The Falsification of the Good*, London: Claridge Press, 1996.

dental negation, a supreme 'nay-saying' to the human condition to which there is and can be no merely human rejoinder. In this society there is only power, and the goal of power is power. In the place where love should be there is an absence; in the place of law another absence; in place of obligation, friendship, responsibility and right, only absence. Truth is what power decides, and reality no more than a construct of power. People can be 'vaporized' – for their existence was never more than provisional, a momentary arrest in the flow of unmeaning. Language has been turned against itself, so that the attempt to mean something will always fail. Newspeak deconstructs the word, so that nothing speaks (or writes) in it save power. And ruling through this power is a supreme cleverness, the Mephistophelian irony of O'Brien, who undermines in his rhetoric the very system that he serves, mockingly enforcing through torture the view that torture, like everything else, is utterly pointless. The machine of *1984* smoothly and infallibly places a negation sign before every meaning, every value, every comprehensible, lovable and all-too-human thing.

Besançon doesn't explicitly say that this system is the work of the Devil. But that is what he implies. For we are unable to accept that this utter negation of human values, hopes and emotions should arise by an 'invisible hand'. Or rather, we can explain it in such a way, but only by ceasing to understand it. Even in the 'impersonal' evil of *1984* or the death camp, therefore, we are brought face to face with the metaphysical character of evil – its character, so to speak, as a 'will towards nothingness'. The negation of the human soul invariably strikes us as a kind of *project*, and we irresistibly imagine a will, a purpose and a hatred of creation behind its grim devices.

Furthermore, these forms of systematic evil are also supreme examples of the power of temptation. Solzhenitsyn, faced with the Soviet system, responded with the prayer: 'Let it not be through *me* that evil enters the world'. But the answer to that prayer, he showed, is merely a higher order of suffering – imprisonment, exile, even murder. For the system will accept only those who compromise, who relinquish justice, trust and love, and who prepare themselves at every moment to betray their neighbours.

Again, Orwell foretold this. In *1984*, conformity to the regime requires not custom or habit but a readiness to betray everything, even that – especially that – which is loved.

I shall give a minor example of what I have in mind, since it is one with which I have been brought into contact in my own life. The first act of the communists after seizing power in Czechoslovakia was to put all those who had exhibited patriotic loyalty on trial for 'treason'. Those who had served so bravely and effectively with the Czech Air Force in the Battle of Britain, for example, were arrested and sentenced to long terms of hard labour in the uranium mines, from which few of them emerged. Similar treatment was meted out to those who had fought to liberate their country from the Germans. Collaborators were welcomed into the party; patriots were excluded. The Foreign Minister in the post-war Social Democrat government was found guilty of treason for her attempts to defend the independence of the Czechs and Slovaks against communist subversion. She was hanged, and her unborn child died inside her on the gallows. The punishing of loyalty went hand in hand with the rewarding of betrayal. Thus it came about, by the end of the communist regime, that one household in every five contained someone who was reporting to the secret police. And in all other households the benefits of housing, education, hospital treatment or travel could be obtained only by a general readiness to act against the demands of conscience. To live a normal life was automatically to give way to temptation.[93] Such, it is natural to assume, is the Devil's work.

To say that the Devil, invoked in this way, is merely a metaphor, is to repeat the problem, not to solve it. For why is it that just *this* metaphor intrudes upon our language, when we try to do justice to the facts? The question parallels that of human freedom. From the standpoint of biological science, freedom too may seem like a metaphor: but the concept is forced upon us by life itself, as we strive to relate to each other as human beings. It

---

93   I have tried to convey the quotidian reality of this situation in 'The Seminar', in *A Dove Descending and Other Stories*, London: Sinclair-Stevenson, 1991.

is, in my view, the greatest of Kant's insights, to have recognized that we are compelled by the very effort of communication to treat each other not as mere organisms or things, but as persons, who are rationally accountable and who must be treated as ends in themselves. And even if we think Kant's theory of freedom to be a metaphysical error, there is no denying the phenomenon that it attempts to explain. Likewise we may dismiss this or that theological theory of evil, as fraught with unwarranted metaphysical assumptions. But the phenomenon *itself* is metaphysical – not *of* this world, though *in* it – and this compels us to describe it as we do.

Perhaps it is easier to grasp this point if we return from the systematic and impersonal-seeming evils of modern totalitarianism, and return to the idea from which I began – that of the evil person. It is characteristic of our loss of the theological perspective that we tend to see evil in terms of suffering. The evil person, we think, is motivated by hatred, and desires to inflict pain, injury, fear and distress on his victim. The idea of 'evil pleasures' has slipped from our grasp. But it is through pleasure, power and glory that Mephistopheles tempts the soul of Faust. And perhaps our most vivid experiences of personal evil are granted to us in the context of sexual pleasure, when desire overrides, disregards or violates the freedom of its object.

Charm is never so apparent as in the words and gestures of the seducer. Sexual liberation has made us reluctant to describe this charm as evil, at least when deployed between 'consenting adults in private'. But it is often experienced as evil by the victim. This fact has been brought home by a striking recent development. As sexual conduct has been liberated from traditional constraints, women have begun to level new and hitherto unknown accusations against the men who try to seduce them. 'Sexual harrassment' is suddenly ubiquitous in Western societies, even though it was unknown or unrecorded only 20 years ago. And women who consent to sex now frequently cry 'rape' thereafter. 'Date rape' is even beginning to be recognized in America as a distinct offence in law. Charges of date rape are brought by women who feel they have been damaged by an encounter to which they nevertheless ostensibly consented. No doubt many of these charges are exploitative and unjust. But the mere fact that they exist, and that they are often put forward with urgency and conviction by women who in no way mean to deny the momentary pleasure that gave rise to them, suggests that liberation has not destroyed the old experience of sexual danger. And the danger cannot be understood, I believe, without the concept of evil.

Mozart gives expression to the seducer's charm in *Don Giovanni*, and contrives a suitable theological punishment. He portrays the damage done by seduction in the distraught Donna Anna and the lamenting Donna Elvira; and he matchlessly shows charm in action, in the duet between Don Giovanni and Zerlina, '*La ci darem*'. But the music is so brilliantly shaped by the Don's desire, that we too are charmed by it. We witness the damage done by Don Giovanni's deep-down indifference to his victims, and conclude that there is something Mephistophelian at work in him. It is true that the Don's victims escape from him, if not *virgo intacto*, at least *anima intacta*; but this comic aspect is due not to any virtue in the seducer, but to the supreme moral vigilance of Mozart's music, which will not allow seduction to have the final say.

On the other hand, we should not doubt that in seduction the soul or self may be jeopardized. Were it not so, then rape would be a minor crime, and 'date rape' no crime at all. It is because a woman is damaged in her sense of self that the experience of 'date rape' is so traumatic. The victim will often feel shamed, humiliated, her sexuality sullied and spoiled. Something has been stolen from her, and this thing is not her body, but herself. All those commonplace descriptions will be dismissed by the sceptic as metaphors, and once again I reply that these are the descriptions that the experience itself may compel, and it is up to us to make sense of them. They demand a metaphysical exegesis, and the place to begin this exegesis is by examining the state of mind of the seducer. For the violated woman frequently describes her experience as an encounter with evil.

This experience of evil is not an experience of physical hurt or pain; on the contrary, it may have arisen from the most intense physical pleasure. It takes the form of a sudden revulsion, as the victim perceives that her freedom and self-hood have fallen into alien hands. The work of negation has been wrought, not on her body, conceived as a merely physical thing, but on her *embodiment* – on her sense of her body as the physical outreach of the self. At a certain moment the seducer appears in his true light. He is not, his victim realizes, taking pleasure *with* me, but *on* me and *against* me. His pleasure appears bestial and the victim too is transfigured in her own eyes into something bestial.

The explanation of these sentiments lies in sexual desire itself. Desire is an elaborate artefact, with which our growth as persons is entwined. Unlike the reproductive urges of animals, human sexual emotion is a kind of language, the vehicle of a moral dialogue, and like any language it is socially taught. And in order that it be shaped as a language, desire must be withheld, rescued from the realm of animal urges and re-fashioned as a moral choice. Hence desire is surrounded by shame and hesitation – by what Scheler calls a *Schutzgefühl*, or protective emotion,[94] whose function is to safeguard its inter-personal goal.

What is wanted by the true lover is a reciprocal self-giving, the focus of which is the other person, conceived as a conscious subject. Through physical tenderness I 'incarnate the other' in his body, as Sartre puts it,[95] and I have tried elsewhere to give the full metaphysical picture that makes sense of Sartre's imagery.[96] But not all desire is normal desire. Because desire is an artefact it may be mis-constructed. For example, it may be directed away from the person to the body, conceived as a kind of sex-machine. Desire can target those who have not learned its language, and – by stimulating them to sexual pleasure without the possibility of mutual giving – can destroy the capacity for true sexual union.

The seducer is avoiding the relation that his victim offers. The victim is making a gift of herself, and he is not refusing that gift

94 Max Scheler, *Uber Scham und Schamgefühl*, in *Schriften aus dem Nachlass*, second edn, ed. Maria Scheler, Bern: Francke, 1957.
95 *Being and Nothingness*, p. 398.
96 R. Scruton, *Sexual Desire: A Philosophical Investigation*, London: Weidenfeld & Nicolson, 1986.

but pretending not to perceive it. In his eyes the transaction is for pleasure only, and any relation to his victim must be free of all obligations beyond the moment. But when the self is given and received, obligations follow automatically. In order not to receive the gift, therefore, the seducer must look through it as though it were not there. It is when his victim realizes that he is not looking *at* her but *through* her that desire turns to disgust.[97]

At the same time, to obtain his goal, the seducer must pretend to the utmost tenderness and solicitation. He may even be taken in by his own pretence, carried away like Don Giovanni by senti-mental passion, towards a momentary idealization of its object – though an idealization that lasts only so long as the present excitement. This too is matchlessly conveyed by Mozart, and is clearly in Kierkegaard's mind, in his striking account of Mozart's opera.[98] In a way, this self-captivation redeems Mozart's Don: he is like a string of momentary selves, each of them wholly given to the woman of the moment, but each of them dying with the moment's lust. The Don escapes from evil into the condition that has been called eroticism:[99] the mutual exaltation of lovers, in and through their desire. His full engagement with his victim elicits an equal response, as in a mirror. And although Don Giovanni refuses love this refusal, when it comes, is the gesture of another self – one who has stepped into the place vacated by the original seducer, who died in the moment of orgasm.

The ordinary seducer is less of an artist. Evil comes because the gift of self is coolly and calculatingly withheld, even in the act of seduction. The evil seducer acts so as to coax the gift of self, only to pollute that gift and re-make it as something wasted. He leaves his victim with the image of a sordid transaction, a generalized dealing with her body, in which she herself has been robbed and

97   See also Sartre's penetrating description of the look, as part of the language of desire: *op. cit.*, p. 393ff.
98   S. Kierkegaard, 'The Immediate Stages of the Erotic', in *Either/Or*, trs. D. F. Swenson and L. M. Swenson, New York: Anchor Books, 1959.
99   For example by Denis de Rougemont, *L'Amour et l'Occident*, Paris: Plon, 1939, and Octavio Paz, *La Llama Doble: Amor y Erotismo*, Mexico City: Seix Barral, 1993.

discarded. Her body has been made corpse-like and obscene. The seducer hopes to avoid creating this perception. But it is a true perception of what he is actually and intentionally doing. He too is a 'spirit that denies', and what he negates is precisely that which Mephistopheles negates, namely the soul of his victim.

That description of sexual evil is only a first step towards an analysis, and is perhaps too phenomenological to carry objective conviction. I am drawn to it, however, for two reasons. First, because it helps to explain a well-known but otherwise puzzling phenomenon – which is that of the devastation caused by bad sexual encounters. Second, because it corresponds to my paradigm of the evil person, as I painted him in the early part of this chapter. I venture to suggest that for many people, their most vivid and perhaps only encounters with evil have been in the sexual context. Those abused as children, those subjected to incestuous advances, those targeted by predatory or ruthless seducers, those who have come away from sex with a dawning sense of violation – all these are traumatized not physically but spiritually, and look on their abusers with the same icy hatred that Faust turns at last on Mephistopheles. And, I suspect, most of them do not see their abusers merely as bad people, with whom they can establish ordinary and forgiving relations, but as people set apart, who visit our world from the realm of anti-spirit, to prey like vampires on human flesh.

If I am right, however, we should not be surprised, either by the tendency to give a theological account of evil, or by the fact that sex has played such an important part in traditional conceptions of the evil side of human nature. The medievals were not entirely deluded, it seems to me, in thinking that sex is the gate through which the Devil enters our lives, or that this gate must always be defended. And, having left it undefended – indeed, having devoted much time and energy to making it indefensible – we should not be surprised, looking around us, at the enormous burden of human unhappiness, or the breakdown of trust between the sexes. Indeed, we ought to be more prepared to admit, what we are nevertheless reluctant to admit, since we ourselves are so much to blame for it, that the institutionalized betrayal foretold by Orwell, which came into being by force in the Soviet Empire, has come into being by consent in the West. In one case the cause was a desire to destroy God; in the other case it is a failure to perceive Him.

11

Eliot and Conservatism

T. S. Eliot was indisputably the greatest poet writing in English in the twentieth century; he was also the most revolutionary Anglophone literary critic since Johnson, and the most influential religious thinker in the Anglican tradition since the Wesleyan movement. His social and political vision is contained in all his writings, and has been absorbed and re-absorbed by generations of English and American readers – upon whom it exerts an almost mystical fascination, even when they are moved, as many are, to reject it. Without Eliot, the philosophy of Toryism would have lost all substance during the last century. And, while not explicitly intending it, he set this philosophy on a higher plane, intellectually, spiritually and stylistically, than has ever been achieved by the socialist idea.

Eliot was born in St Louis, Missouri, in 1888, and educated at Harvard, the Sorbonne and Merton College, Oxford, where he wrote a doctoral thesis on the philosophy of F. H. Bradley, whose Hegelian vision of society exerted a profound influence over him. He came, as did so many educated Americans of his generation, from a profoundly religious and public-spirited background, although his early poems suggest a bleak and despairing agnosticism, which he only gradually and painfully overcame. In 1914 he met Ezra Pound, who encouraged him to settle in England. He married during the following year, which also saw the publication of his first successful poem, 'The Love Song of J. Alfred Prufrock'. This work, together with the other short poems which were published along with it as *Prufrock and Other Observations* in 1917, profoundly altered the course of English literature. They were the first truly *modernist* works in English; and the most visible influences on their imagery and diction were not English but French – specifically, the *fin-de-siècle* irony of Laforgue, and the symbolism of Rimbaud, Mallarmé and Verlaine. They were also social poems, concerned to express a prevailing collective mood, even when dressed in the words of a specific protagonist. The generation that had marched to the Front with *A Shropshire Lad* in their knapsacks, returned (if they were lucky) to find their altered condition reflected in these poems, which were poems of isolation and anxiety, with a disillusioned refusal to mourn.

Shortly afterwards Eliot published a book of essays – *The Sacred Wood* – which was to be as influential as the early poetry. Eliot presented, in these essays, his new and exacting theory of the role of criticism, and of the necessity for criticism if our literary culture is to survive. For Eliot it is no accident that criticism and poetry so often come together in the same intelligence – as in his own case, and the case of Coleridge, whom he singled out as the finest of English critics. For the critic, like the poet, is concerned to develop the 'sensibility' of his reader – by which term Eliot intended a kind of intelligent observation of the human world. Critics do not abstract or generalize: they *look*, and record what they see. But in doing so, they also convey a sense of what *matters* in human experience, distinguishing the false from the genuine emotion. While Eliot was to spell out only gradually and obscurely over many years just what he meant by 'sensibility', his elevated conception of the critic's role struck a chord in many of his readers. Furthermore, *The Sacred Wood* contained essays that were to revolutionize literary taste. The authoritative tone of these essays, and their rejection of the sentimental romanticism of so many of Eliot's contemporaries, gave rise to the impression that the modern world was at last making itself heard in literature, and that its voice was T. S. Eliot's.

The Sacred Wood turned the attention of the literary world away from romantic literature, towards the 'metaphysical poets' of the sixteenth and seventeenth centuries, and towards the Elizabethan dramatists – the lesser predecessors and heirs of

Shakespeare – whose raw language, rich with the sensation of the thing described, provided a telling contrast to the sentimental sweetness that Eliot condemned in his immediate contemporaries. There is also an essay on Dante, discussing the question that was frequently to trouble Eliot, of the relation between poetry and belief. To what extent could one appreciate the poetry of the *Divine Comedy* while rejecting the doctrine that had inspired it? This question was a real one for Eliot, for the following reasons. First, he was (like his fellow modernists and contemporaries, Pound and Joyce) profoundly influenced by Dante, whose limpid verse-form, colloquial style and solemn philosophy created a vision of the ideal in poetry. At the same time, Eliot rejected the theological vision of the *Divine Comedy* – rejected it with a deep sense of loss. Yet, in his own poetry, the voice of Dante would constantly return, offering him turns of phrase, lightning flashes of thought and a vision of the modern world from a point of view outside it, a point of view irradiated by an experience of holiness – although an experience that Eliot did not share. And when he *did* finally come to share in this vision, or at least to acknowledge his own conversion to Christianity, he wrote, in the last of *Four Quartets*, the most brilliant of all imitations of Dante in English – an imitation that is something far finer than an imitation, in which the religious vision of Dante is transported and translated into the world of modern England.

One other essay in *The Sacred Wood* deserves mention: 'Tradition and the Individual Talent', in which Eliot introduces the term that best summarizes his contribution to the political consciousness of our century – 'tradition'. In this essay Eliot argues that true originality is possible only within a tradition, and that every tradition must be re-made by the original artist, in the very act of creating something new. A tradition is a living thing, and just as each writer is judged in terms of those who went before, so does the meaning of the tradition change, as new works are added to it. Briefly, it was this literary idea of a live tradition that was gradually to permeate Eliot's thinking, and form the core of his social and political philosophy.

Prufrock and *The Sacred Wood* already help us to understand the paradox of T. S. Eliot – that our greatest modernist should also be our greatest modern conservative. The man who over-threw the nineteenth century in literature and inaugurated the age of free verse, alienation and experiment was also the man who, in 1928, was to describe himself as 'classical in literature, royalist in politics, and Anglo-Catholic in religion'.[100] This seeming paradox contains the clue to Eliot's stature as a social and political thinker. For he perceived that it is precisely in modern conditions – conditions of fragmentation, heresy and unbelief – that the conservative project acquires its sense. Con-servatism is itself a modernism, and in this lies the secret of its success. What distinguishes Burke from the French revolution-aries is not his attachment to things past, but his desire to live fully in the present, to understand it in all its imperfections, and to accept it as the only reality that is offered to us. Like Burke, Eliot recognized the distinction between a backward-looking nostalgia, which is but another form of modern sentimentality, and a genuine tradition, which grants us the courage and the vision with which to live in the modern world.

In 1922 Eliot founded a literary quarterly, *The Criterion*, which he continued to edit until 1939, when he closed the journal down under the pressure of 'depression of spirits' induced by 'the present state of public affairs'. As the title of the journal suggests, the project was animated by Eliot's sense of the importance of criticism, and of the futility of modernist experiments when not informed by literary judgement, moral seriousness and a sense of the importance of the written word. The journal also contained social philosophy of a conservative persuasion – although Eliot preferred the word 'classicism' as a description of its outlook. *The Criterion* was the forum in which much of our modernist litera-ture was first published – including the poetry of Pound, Empson, Auden and Spender. Its first issue contained the work which established Eliot himself as the greatest poet of his generation: *The Waste Land*. This seemed to its first readers fully to capture

---

100 *For Lancelot Andrewes*, another of his path-breaking collections of essays, London: Faber & Gwyer, 1928.

the disillusionment and emptiness that followed the hollow victory of the First World War – a conflict in which European civilization had committed suicide, as Greek civilization had in the Peloponnesian War. Yet the work hardly mentioned the war, had none of the vivid imagery of battle that English readers knew from the works of Wilfred Owen and Siegfried Sassoon and was chock-a-block with references to and quotations from a scholar's library. Its ostensible subject matter was drawn from works of armchair anthropology – in particular *The Golden Bough* of Sir James Frazer, a work which provided the title of *The Sacred Wood*; and *From Ritual to Romance* by Jessie Weston, in which Frazerian ideas are applied to medieval literature.

The Waste Land was re-published, with notes in which Eliot explains some of the references and allusions – in particular that contained in the title, which alludes to the 'Fisher King' of the Parsifal legend, who presides over a waste land, awaiting the hero who will ask the questions that will destroy winter's bleak enchantment and renew the world. The allegory of modern civilization contained in this reference to the medieval fertility cults and their literary transformation in Arthurian romance was not lost on Eliot's readers. Nor was it the first time that these symbols and legends of medieval romance had been put to such a use – witness Wagner's *Parsifal*, to which Eliot refers obliquely by quoting from Verlaine's poem. Nevertheless, there was a peculiar poignancy in the very erudition of the poem – as though the whole of Western culture were being brought to bear on the desert landscape of the modern city, in a last effort to encompass it, to internalize it and to understand its meaning. The use of anthropological conceptions parallels Wagner's use of the teutonic myths. (There are in *The Waste Land* more quotations from Wagner than from any other poet.) Eliot is invoking the religious worldview – and in particular the sense that life's renewal depends upon supernatural forces – but as a fact about human consciousness, rather than an item of religious belief. In this way, he was able to avail himself of religious ideas and imagery, without committing himself to any religious belief. Yet, as he was rapidly discovering, without religious ideas and imagery, the true

A Political Philosophy

condition of the modern world could not be described. For it must be described from a point of view outside history, with which to grasp the extent of our spiritual loss.

After *The Waste Land* Eliot continued to write poetry inspired by the agonizing dissociation, as he saw it, between the sensibility of our culture and the available experience of the modern world. This phase of his development culminated in a profound Christian statement – the poem *Ash-Wednesday*, in which he abandoned his anthropological manner, and announced his conversion to the Anglo-Catholic faith. By now Eliot was ready to take up his own peculiar cross – which was the cross of membership. No longer playing the part of spiritual and political exile, he threw in his lot with the tradition to which his favourite authors had belonged. He became a British citizen, joined the Anglican Church and wrote his striking verse drama, *Murder in the Cathedral*, about the meaning of Christian martyrdom and about the long-drawn-out conflict between Church and State, of which the Anglo-Catholic settlement had been the eventual solution. In a series of essays, he praised the writings of Anglican sixteenth-century divines, and attacked the humanism and the secular heresies of his time. This phase of Eliot's development culminated in *After Strange Gods*, a 'primer of modern heresy', in which he expressed his conservative antipathy to secular doctrine. This essay has long been out of print, since passing remarks contained in it have drawn the charge (whether or not justified) of anti-Semitism, and Eliot's estate has therefore preferred not to revive the controversy. It was the first of several attempts at social philosophy, of which the two most famous are *The Idea of a Christian Society*, published in 1940, and *Notes Towards the Definition of Culture*, published in 1948. Both these works are marked by a tentativeness and anxiety about the new condition of Europe, which make them far less clear guides to Eliot's vision than the great poem which he wrote at the same time, and which has been, for many of my generation, the essential account of our spiritual crisis, and the greatest message of hope that has been given to us. This poem – *Four Quartets* – is a profound exploration of spiritual possibilities, in which the poet seeks and finds the vision outside time in which time and history are redeemed. It is a religious work, and at the same time a work of extraordinary lyric power, like the *Cimetière marin* of Valéry, but vastly more mature in its underlying philosophy.

In addition to those works, Eliot is of abiding significance for his attempt to revive the verse play as a literary medium. His *Family Reunion* (1939) explores the theme of inherited guilt, drawing, as did *Murder in the Cathedral*, on the central devices of Greek tragedy. These impressive dramas were followed by three verse comedies, which elevate the conventions of the London drawing-room theatre to a new artistic height. Eliot continued to write the essays which re-drew the map of English literature, and added to his poetic achievement the famous and skilful book of children's verse – *Old Possum's Book of Practical Cats* – 'Possum' being the name given to Eliot by Ezra Pound, to commemorate Eliot's habit of lying, like a possum, out of sight.

His life began with a question – the question of modern life and its meaning – and his work was a long, studious and sincere attempt to provide an answer. In the course of this enterprise, he re-shaped the English language, changed the forms of English verse and produced some of the most memorable utterances in our literature. Although an impressive scholar, with a mastery of languages and literatures that he reveals but does not oppressively dwell upon in his writings, Eliot was also a man of the world. He worked first as a teacher (in my old grammar school), then in a London bank and then in the publishing house of Faber and Faber, which he made into the foremost publisher of poetry and criticism in its day. His unhappy first marriage did not impede his active participation in the literary life of London, over which he exerted an influence every bit as great as André Breton over the literary life of Paris. And his refusal, through all this, to adopt the mantle of the bohemian, to claim the tinsel crown of artist or to mock the 'bourgeois' lifestyle sets him apart from the continental tradition which he did so much to promote. He realized that the true task of the artist in the modern world is one not of repudia-tion but of reconciliation. The 'enfant-térrible-ism' of a Cocteau or the anti-bourgeois aggression of a Sartre were entirely foreign to him. For Eliot the artist inherits, in heightened and self-conscious form, the very same anxieties that are the stuff of ordinary experience. The poet who takes words seriously is the voice of mankind, interceding for those who live around him, and gaining on their behalf the gift of consciousness with which to overcome the wretchedness of secular life. He too is an ordinary bourgeois, and his highest prize is to live unnoticed amid those who know nothing of his art – as the saint may live unnoticed among those for whom he dies.

To find the roots of Eliot's political thinking, we must go back to the modernism that found such striking expression in *The Waste Land*. English literature in the early part of the twentieth century – and English poetry in particular – was to a great extent captured by pre-modern imagery, by references to a form of life (such as we find in Thomas Hardy) that had vanished for ever and by verse forms which derived from the repertoire of romantic isolation. It had not undergone that extraordinary education which Baudelaire and his sucessors had imposed upon the French – in which antiquated forms like the sonnet were wrenched free of their pastoral and religious connotation, and fitted out with the language of the modern city. Baudelaire's use of the sonnet conveys the new and hallucinating sense of an irreparable fault, whereby modern man is divided from all that has preceded him. Eliot's admiration for Baudelaire arose from his desire to write verse that was as true to the experience of the modern city as Baudelaire's had been to the experience of Paris. He summed up his admiration for the French poet thus: 'It is not merely in the use of imagery of common life, not merely in the use of imagery of the sordid life of a great metropolis, but in the elevation of such imagery to the *first* intensity – presenting it as it is, and yet making it represent something much more than itself – that Baudelaire has created a mode of release and expression for other men'.[101] Eliot also recognized in Baudelaire the new character of the religious impulse, in the conditions of modern life. 'The important fact about Baudelaire,' he wrote, ' is that he was essen-

---

101   *Selected Essays*, London: Faber & Faber, 1932, p. 426.

tially a Christian, born out of his due time, and a classicist, born out of his due time.'[102]

Eliot's complaint against the neo-Romantic literature of his day was not merely a literary complaint. He believed that its use of worn out poetic diction and lilting rhythms betrayed a serious moral weakness: a failure to observe life as it really is, a failure to feel what must be felt towards the experience that is inescapably ours. And this failure is not confined, he believed, to literature, but runs through the whole of modern life. The search for a new idiom is therefore part of a larger search, for the reality of modern experience. Only then can we confront our situation and ask ourselves what should be done about it. Eliot's deep distrust of secular humanism – and of the socialist and democratic ideas of society which he believed to stem from it – reflected his critique of the neo-Romantics. The humanist, with his myth of man's goodness, is taking refuge in an easy falsehood. He is living in a world of make-believe, trying to avoid the real emotional cost of seeing things as they are. His vice is the vice of Edwardian and 'Georgian' poetry – the vice of sentimentality, which causes us not merely to speak and write in clichés, but to *feel* in clichés too, lest we should be troubled by the truth of our condition. The task of the artistic modernist, as he later expressed it, borrowing a phrase from Mallarmé, is 'to purify the dialect of the tribe': that is, to find the words, rhythms and artistic forms that would make contact again with our experience – not my experience, or yours, but *our* experience – the experience that unites us as living here and now. And it is only because he had captured this experience – in particular, in the bleak vision of *The Waste Land* – that Eliot was able to find a path to its meaning.

He summarizes his attitude to the everyday language of modern life and politics in his essay on Bishop Andrewes, and it is worth quoting the passage in full:

To persons whose minds are habituated to feed on the vague jargon of our time, when we have a vocabulary for every-

---

102   *For Lancelot Andrewes, op. cit.*, p. 77.

thing and exact ideas about nothing – when a word half-understood, torn from its place in some alien or half-formed science, as of psychology, conceals from both writer and reader the utter meaninglessness of a statement, when all dogma is in doubt except the dogmas of sciences of which we have read in the newspapers, when the language of theology itself, under the influence of an undisciplined mysticism of popular philosophy, tends to become a language of tergiversation – Andrewes may seem pedantic and verbose. It is only when we have saturated ourselves in his prose, followed the movement of his thought, that we find his examination of words terminating in the ecstasy of assent. Andrewes takes a word and derives the world from it.[103]

For Eliot, words had begun to lose their precision – not in spite of science but because of it, not in spite of the loss of true religious belief, but because of it, not in spite of the proliferation of technical terms, but because of it. Our modern ways of speaking no longer enable us to 'take a word and derive the world from it': on the contrary, they veil the world, since they convey no lived response to it. They are mere counters in a game of cliché, designed to fill up the silence, to conceal the void which has come as the old gods have departed from their haunts among us. That is why modern ways of thinking are not, as a rule, orthodoxies, but *heresies* – a heresy being a truth that has been exaggerated into falsehood, a truth in which we have taken refuge, so to speak, investing in it all our unexamined anxieties and expecting from it answers to questions that we have not troubled ourselves to understand.[104] In the philosophies that prevail in modern life – utilitarianism, pragmatism, behaviourism – we find that 'words have a habit of changing their meaning . . . or else they are made, in a most ruthless and piratical manner, to walk the plank'.[105] The

103   *For Lancelot Andrewes, op. cit.*, p. 20.
104   *After Strange Gods: A Primer of Modern Heresy*, London: Faber & Faber, 1934.
105   *For Lancelot Andrewes, op. cit.*, p. 67.

same is true, Eliot implies, whenever the humanist heresy takes over – whenever we treat man as god, and believe that our thoughts and our words need be measured by no other standard but themselves.

Eliot was brought up in a democracy and inherited that great fund of public spirit which is the gift of American democracy to the modern world. But he was not a democrat in his feelings. For he believed that culture could not be entrusted to the democratic process, precisely because of this carelessness with words, this habit of unthinking cliché, which would always arise when every person is regarded as having an equal right to express himself. In *The Use of Poetry and the Use of Criticism* he writes:

> When the poet finds himself in an age in which there is no intellectual aristocracy, when power is in the hands of a class so democratized that while still a class it represents itself to be the whole nation; when the only alternatives seem to be to talk to a coterie or soliloquize, the difficulties of the poet and the necessity of criticism become greater.[106]

Hence critics have, for Eliot, an enhanced significance in the modern world. It is they who must act to restore what the aristocratic ideal of taste would otherwise spontaneously generate – a language in which words are used with their full meaning, in order to show the world as it is, without veiling it in a mist of cliché-ridden sentiment. Those nurtured on empty sentiment have no weapons with which to deal with the reality of a god-forsaken world. They fall at once from sentimentality into cynicism, and so lose the power either to experience life or to live with its imperfection.

Eliot therefore perceived an enormous danger in the liberal and 'scientific' humanism which was offered by the prophets of his day. This liberalism seemed to him to be the avatar of moral chaos, since it permits any sentiment to flourish, and deadens all critical judgement with the idea of a democratic right to speak,

---

106   London: Faber & Faber, 1933, second edn, 1964, p. 22.

which becomes insensibly a democratic right to feel. Although 'human kind cannot bear very much reality' – as he expresses the point, first in *Murder in the Cathedral* and then in *Four Quartets* – the purpose of a culture is to retain that elusive thing called 'sensibility': the habit of right feeling. Barbarism ensues, not because people have lost their skills and scientific knowledge; nor is it averted by retaining those things. Barbarism comes through a loss of *culture*, since it is only through culture that the important realities can be truly perceived.

Eliot's thought here is difficult to state precisely. And it is worth drawing a parallel with a thinker whom he disliked: Nietzsche. For Nietzsche, the crisis of modernity had come about because of the loss of the Christian faith. This loss of faith is the inevitable result of science, and of the growth of knowledge. At the same time, it is not possible for human beings really to live without faith; and for us, who have inherited all the habits and concepts of a Christian culture, that faith must be Christianity. Take away the faith and you do not take away a body of doctrine only; nor do you leave a clear uncluttered landscape in which people at last are visible for what they are. You take away the power to perceive other and more important *truths* – truths about our condition which cannot, without the benefit of faith, be properly confronted. (For example: the truth of our mortality; which is not simply a scientific 'fact', to be added to our store of knowledge, but a pervasive *experience* that runs through all things and changes the aspect of the world.)

The solution that Nietzsche impetuously embraced in this quandary was to deny the sovereignty of truth altogether – to say 'there are no truths', and to build a philosophy of life on the ruins of both science and religion, in the name of a purely aesthetic ideal. Eliot saw the absurdity of that response, and the deliberate self-isolation of the man who made it. Yet the paradox remains. The truths that mattered to Eliot are truths of feeling, truths about the *weight* of human life and the reality of human sentiment. Science does not make these truths more easily perceivable: on the contrary, it releases into the human psyche a flock of fantasies – liberalism, humanism, utilitarianism and the rest –

which distract it with the futile hope for a scientific morality. The result is a corruption of the very language of feeling, a decline from sensibility to sentimentality and a veiling of the human world. The paradox, then, is this: the falsehoods of religious faith enable us to perceive the truths that matter. The truths of science, endowed with an absolute authority, hide the truths that matter, and make the human reality imperceivable. Eliot's solution to the paradox was compelled by the path that he had taken to its discovery – the path of poetry, with its agonizing examples of poets whose precision, perception and sincerity were the effects of a Christian belief. The solution was to embrace the Christian faith – not, as Tertullian did, *because* of the paradox, but rather in spite of it.

This explains Eliot's growing conviction that culture and religion are in the last analysis indissoluble.[107] The disease of sentimentality could be overcome, he believed, only by a high culture, in which the work of purification was constantly carried on. This is the task of the critic and the artist, and it is a hard task:

> And so each venture
> Is a new beginning, a raid on the inarticulate
> With shabby equipment always deteriorating
> In the general mess of imprecision of feeling,
> Undisciplined squads of emotion. And what there is
>   to conquer
> By strength and submission, has already been discovered
> Once or twice, or several times, by men whom one
>   cannot hope
> To emulate – but there is no competition –
> There is only the fight to recover what has been lost
> And found and lost again and again: and now, under
>   conditions
> That seem unpropitious . . .[108]

---

107 *Notes Towards the Definition of Culture*, London: Faber & Faber, 1948.
108 'East Coker', *Four Quartets*, London: Faber & Faber, 1943, p. 182.

This work of purification is a dialogue across the generations with those who belong to the tradition: only the few can take part in it, while the mass of mankind strays below, assailed by those 'undisciplined squads of emotion'. The high culture of the few is, however, a moral necessity for the many: for it permits the human reality to *show itself*, and so to guide our conduct. But why should the mass of mankind, lost as they are in bathos, 'distracted from distraction by distraction' be guided by 'those who know' as Dante puts it (*loro chi sanno*)? The answer must lie in religion, and in particular in the common language which a traditional religion bestows, both on the high culture of art, and on the common culture of a people. The religion is the life-blood of a culture. It provides the store of symbols, stories and doctrines that enable us to communicate about our destiny. And it forms, through the sacred texts and liturgies, the constant point to which the poet and the critic can return – the language alike of ordinary believers and of the poets who must confront the ever new conditions of life in the aftermath of knowledge – the life in a fallen world.

For Eliot, however, religion in general and the Christian religion in particular, should not be seen merely in Platonic terms, as an attitude towards what is eternal and unchanging. The truth of our condition is that we are historical beings, who find whatever consolation and knowledge is vouchsafed to us in time. The consolations of religion come to us in temporal costume, through institutions that are alive with the spirit of history. To rediscover our religion is not to rise free from the temporal order; it is not to deny history and corruption, in order to contemplate the timeless truths. On the contrary, it is to enter more deeply into history, so as to find in the merely transitory the mark and the sign of that which never passes: it is to discover the 'point of intersection of the timeless with time', which is, according to *Four Quartets*, the occupation of the saint.

Thus there emerges the strangest and most compelling of parallels: that between the saint and martyr of *Murder in the Cathedral* and the meditating poet of *Four Quartets*. Just as the first brings, through his martyrdom, the light of eternity into the darkness of the people of Canterbury (represented as a chorus of women); so does the poet 'redeem the time', by finding in the stream of time, those timeless moments which point beyond it. And the attempt by the poet to rediscover and belong to a tradition that will give sense and meaning to his language is one with the attempt to find a tradition of belief, of behaviour and of historical allegiance, that will give sense and meaning to the community. The real significance of a religion lies less in the abstract doctrine, than in the institutions which cause it to endure. It lies also in the sacraments and ceremonies, in which the eternal become present and what might have been coincides with what is.

For Eliot, therefore, conversion was not a matter merely of acknowledging the truth of Christ. It involved a conscious gesture of *belonging*, whereby he united his poetical labours with the perpetual labour of the Anglican Church. For the Anglican Church is peculiar in this: that it has never defined itself as 'protestant'; that it has always sought to accept rather than protest against its inheritance, while embracing the daring belief that the truths of Christianity have been offered in a *local* form to the people of England. It is a Church which takes its historical nature seriously, acknowledging that its duty is less to spread the gospel among mankind than to sanctify a specific community. And in order to fit itself for this role, the Anglican Church has, through its divines and liturgists, shaped the English language according to the Christian message, while also bringing that message into the here and now of England. In 'Little Gidding', the last of the *Four Quartets*, the poet finds himself in the village retreat where an Anglican saint had retired to pray with his family. And he conveys what to many is the eternal truth of the Anglican confession, in lines which are among the most famous that have ever been written in English:

> If you came this way,
> Taking any route, starting from anywhere,
> At any time or at any season,
> It would always be the same: you would have to put off
> Sense and notion. You are not here to verify,

> Instruct yourself, or inform curiosity
> Or carry report. You are here to kneel
> Where prayer has been valid. And prayer is more
> Than an order of words, the conscious occupation
> Of the praying mind, or the sound of the voice praying.
> And what the dead had no speech for, when living,
> They can tell you, being dead: the communication
> Of the dead is tongued with fire beyond the language
>   of the living.
> Here, the intersection of the timeless moment
> Is England and nowhere. Never and always.

And later, returning to this theme of communication with the dead – *our* dead – and referring to those brief moments of meaning which are the only sure gift of sensibility, Eliot completes the thought:

> We are born with the dead:
> See, they return, and bring us with them.
> The moment of the rose and the moment of the yew-tree
> Are of equal duration. A people without history
> Is not redeemed from time, for history is a pattern
> Of timeless moments. So, while the light fails
> On a winter's afternoon, in a secluded chapel
> History is now and England.

Much has been written about 'Little Gidding', the atmosphere of which stays in the mind of every cultivated Englishman who reads it. Perhaps it sounds strangely in continental ears – though is there not something, a faint echo perhaps, of Celan in those lines: 'We are born with the dead:/ See, they return, and bring us with them'? What is important, however, is less the atmosphere of the poem, than the thought which advances through it. For here Eliot achieves that for which he envies Dante – namely a poetry of belief, in which belief and words are one, and in which the thought cannot be prized free from the measured language. Moreover, there is one influence throughout which is inescapable

– the King James Bible, and the Anglican liturgy that grew alongside it. Without being consciously biblical, and while using only modern and colloquial English, Eliot endows his verse with the authority of liturgy, and with the resonance of faith.

Moreover, those very lines take us back to the core belief of modern conservatism, the belief in the Burkean contract between the living, the dead and the unborn. And, Burke implied, it is only those who listen to the dead who are the fit guardians of the unborn. Eliot's complex theory of tradition gives sense and form to this idea. For he makes clear that the most important thing that future generations must inherit from us is culture. Culture is the repository of an experience which is at once local and placeless, present and timeless, the experience of a community as sanctified by time. This we pass on, only if we, too, inherit it. And, therefore, we must listen to the voices of the dead and capture their meaning in those brief, elusive moments when 'History is now and England'. Only in a religious community are such moments part of everyday life. For us, in the modern world, religion and culture are both to be *gained* through a work of sacrifice. But it is a sacrifice upon which everything depends. Hence, by an extraordinary route, the modernist poet becomes the traditionalist priest: and the stylistic achievement of the first is one with the spiritual achievement of the second.

To many people, Eliot's theory of culture and tradition is too arduous, and imposes an impossible duty upon the educated elite. To others, however, it has been a vital inspiration. For let us ask ourselves just what is required, of 'those who know'. Should they, in the modern world, devote themselves like Sartre or Foucault to undermining the 'structures' of bourgeois society, to scoffing at manners and morals and ruining the institutions upon which they depend for their exalted status? Should they play the part of a modern Socrates, questioning everything and affirming nothing? Should they go along with the culture of play, the postmodernist fantasy world in which all is permitted since neither permitting nor forbidding make sense? To answer 'Yes' to any of those questions is in effect to live by negation, to grant nothing to human life beyond the mockery of it. It is to inaugurate and endorse the new world of 'transgression', a world that will not reproduce itself, since it will undermine the very motive which causes a society to reproduce. The conservative response to modernity is to embrace it, but to embrace it *critically*, in full consiousness that human achievements are rare and precarious, that we have no God-given right to destroy our inheritance, but must always patiently submit to the voice of order, and set an example of orderly living. The future of mankind, for the socialist, is simple: pull down the existing order and allow the future to emerge. But it will not emerge, as we know. These philosophies of the 'new world' are lies and delusions, products of a sentimentality which has veiled the facts of human nature. We can do nothing, unless we first amend ourselves. The task is to re-discover the world which made us, to see ourselves as part of something greater, which depends upon *us* for its survival, and which still can live in us, provided we achieve that 'condition of complete simplicity/ (Costing not less than everything)', to which Eliot directs us.

> We shall not cease from exploration
> And the end of all our exploring
> Will be to arrive where we started
> And know the place for the first time.[109]

Such is the conservative message for our times, and it is a message beyond politics, a message of liturgical weight and authority – but a message that must be received, if humane and moderate politics is to remain a possibility.

---

109   'Little Gidding', *Four Quartets*, London: Faber & Faber, 1942.

Acknowledgements

1. Conserving Nations. A longer version of this chapter was published by the London think-tank Civitas in 2004, as a pamphlet entitled *The Need for Nations*. I am grateful to David Green and Civitas for their permission to reuse the material.

2. Conserving Nature. This chapter is reprinted from Andy Dobson and Robyn Eckersley (eds), *Political Theory and the Ecological Challenge*, Cambridge: CUP, 2006.

3. Eating our Friends. This chapter is an expanded version of 'The Conscientious Carnivore', published in Steve F. Sapontzis (ed.), *Food for Thought: The Debate over Eating Meat*, Amherst, NY: Prometheus, 2004. I am grateful to Steve Sapontzis and Prometheus Books for the permission to reprint.

4. Dying Quietly. This chapter is based on a lecture delivered to the Honourable Society of the Inner Temple in 2005, and published in the *Inner Temple Yearbook* for that year. I wish to thank the Master and Benchers of the Inn for the invitation to talk to the Society.

5. Meaningful Marriage. This chapter was first published in Robert P. George and Jean Bethke Elshtain (eds), *The Meaning of Marriage*, New York: Spence Publishing, 2006.

6. Extinguishing the Light. This chapter was delivered as a lecture in response to the award of the Ingersoll Prize for 2004.

7. Religion and Enlightenment. This chapter was delivered in a conference on the place of religion in modern societies, organized in 2003 in Princeton by the Witherspoon Institute. I am grateful to Dan Dennett for subsequent comments.

8. The Totalitarian Temptation. This chapter was delivered in a conference on totalitarianism organized by the University of Krakow in 2003.

9. Newspeak and Eurospeak. This chapter was delivered in a conference on language organized by the Engleberg Forum at Lausanne in Switzerland, summer 2005.

10. The Nature of Evil. This chapter was delivered in a conference organized in 2003 by the Nexus Institute in the University of Tilburg.

11. Eliot and Conservatism. This chapter was delivered as a lecture in the Masaryk University, Brno, in 2000.

Name Index

Subject Index